قواعد اللغة الإنكليزية

قواعد اللغة الإنكليزية

إعداد وإشراف

محمد أحمد

مكتبة حسن العصرية
للطباعة والنشر والتوزيع
بيروت - لبنان

مكتبة حسن العصرية
للطباعة والنشر والتوزيع
بيروت - لبنان

الطبعة الأولى	:	1432هـ / 2011م
اسم الكتاب	:	قواعد اللغة الإنكليزية
إعداد وإشراف	:	محمد أحمد
إخراج وتصميم	:	غنى الريس الشحيمي
عدد الصفحات	:	400 صفحة
قياس	:	17 × 24
الناشر	:	مكتبة حسن العصرية
العنوان	:	بيروت- كورنيش المزرعة- الحسن سنتر- بلوك B- الطابق 4
صندوق البريد	:	6501- 14 بيروت – لبنان
هاتف خليوي	:	00961 3 790520
تلفاكس	:	00961 7 920452
		00961 1 306951
الترقيم الدولي	:	978-9953-561-07-3
البريد الإلكتروني	:	E-mail: library.hasansaad@hotmail.com

Printed in Lebanon 2011 طبع في لبنان

الدرس الأول

الحروف الأبجدية الإنجليزية

English Alphabets

حرف كبير مطبعي		حرف صغير مطبعي		حرف كتابي كبير	حرف صغير كتابي		اللفظ في كلمة
A	ei	a	ei	A	a	آي	hat-cap
B	bi	b	bi	B	b	بي	bad-bat
C	si	c	si	C	c	سي	cinema
D	di	d	di	D	d	دي	do-does
E	i	e	i	E	e	إ	let-best
F	ef	f	ef	F	f	أّف	fat-fit
G	gi	g	gi	G	g	جي	go-bag
H	etch	h	etch	H	h	أتش	he-how
I	ai	i	ai	I	i	آي	it-pin
J	gei	j	gei	J	j	جَاي	jam-joy
K	kei	k	kei	K	k	كآي	kind-key
L	el	l	el	L	l	أّل	land-lank
M	em	m	em	M	m	أّم	madam
N	en	n	en	N	n	أّن	no-in
O	ou	o	ou	O	o	آو	hot-rock
P	pi	p	pi	P	p	پـي	paper
Q	kiu	q	kiu	Q	q	كيو	quake
R	ar	r	ar	R	r	آر	run-try
S	es	s	es	S	s	أّس	say-yes
T	ti	t	ti	T	t	تي	tell-it
U	iu	u	iu	U	u	يُو	ful-put
V	vi	v	vi	V	v	ڤـي	very-save
W	dable iu	w	dable iu	W	w	دَبليو	will-wife
X	ix	x	ix	X	x	إكس	x-ray
Y	uai	y	uai	Y	y	واي	yacht-yell
Z	zed	z	zed	Z	z	زّد	zeal-zero

إن عدد الحروف الإنجليزية (26) حرفاً منها (5) حروف متحركة أو صائتة والباقي حروف ساكنة (صحيحة) (Consonants).

الحروف المتحركة: (حروف العلة): The Vowels are as follows: هي الآتي: (a- e- i- o- u)

إن كل اسم يبدأ بصوت أحد هذه الحروف الخمس المذكورة أعلاه في حالة المفرد لا بدّ أن تسبقه أداة النكرة وهي (an)، بينما كل اسم يبدأ بحرف من الحروف الساكنة وعددها (21) حرفاً لا بدّ أن تسبقه أداة النكرة وهي (a) في حالة المفرد فقط، وجمع الحرفين المذكورين (an, a) هي كلمة (some) وتعني (بعض) وعكسها (any).

الأسماء التي تبدأ بالحروف المتحرّكة مثل:

(واحة)	an oasis	
تفاحة	It is an apple.	an apple
بيضةٌ	It is an egg.	an egg
محبرةٌ	It is an inkpot.	an inkpot
برتقالةٌ	It is an orange.	an orange
مظلةٌ	It is an umbrella	an umbrella

(Consonants)		الأسماء التي تبدأ بالحروف الساكنة مثل:	
A book	كتاب	A queen	ملكةٌ
A cat	قطة	A room	حجرةٌ
A father	أب	A son	ابنٌ
A mother	أم	A train	قطار
A garden	حديقة	A watch	ساعة جيب/ يد
A paper	ورقة	A yard	ياردة
A key	مفتاح	An x-ray	الأشعة السينية

Exercise (1)

تمرين (1)

Put (a) or (an) before each noun:

ضع أدوات النكرة أو التعريف (ال) أمام كل اسم مذكور أدناه:

book	كتاب	chairs	كراسي
father	أب	eyes	عيون
orange	برتقالة	apples	تفاح
answer	جواب	girl	بنت
eye	عين	classroom	حجرة الدراسة
yard	ياردة	river	نهر
pen	قلم	eggs	بيض
boys	أولاد	oases	واحات (جمع)

الدرس الثاني

الأسماء وأداتا النكرة وأداة التعريف

Nouns and Articles

ينقسم الاسم في اللغة الإنجليزية إلى ثمانية أنواع مختلفة، منها الدالة على أسماء الأشخاص أو لحيوانات أو لعواصم أو لمدن كبيرة أو لجبال أو لأنهار مشهورة في العالم أو لأشياء أخرى. ويُكْتَب الحرف الأول من أسماء العلم بالحرف الكبير Capital Letter.

Proper Nouns (يكتب الحـرف

الأول منها بحرف كبير)

أسماء علم مثل:

Ali – Sami – Nasser – Layla – Nada – Marwa.

علي – سامي – ناصر – ليلى – ندى – مروة.

Nouns of Animals

أسماء لحيوانات

tiger – camel – dog

– cat – hen – horse

– bear – cock – turkey.

نمر – جمل – كلب
– قطة – دجاجة – حصان
– دُب – ديك – ديك رومي.

Nouns Of Capitals

أسماء لعواصم أو لمدن كبيرة مثل:

(يكتب الحرف الأول منها بحرف كبير)

	بيروت
Beirut	

Damascus   دمشق

Tripoli   طرابلس

Cairo   القاهرة

Saida   صيدا

Baghdad   بغداد

Nouns of Mountains

<u>أسماء لجبال مثل:</u>

(يكتب الحرف الأول منها بحرف كبير)

Sanin Mountain	(جبل صنين)	Gibraltar	(جبل طارق)
Mount Everest	(جبل أفرست)	Atlas Mountains	(جبال الأطلس)

Nouns Of Rivers & Canals

<u>أسماء لأنهار ولقنوات</u>

(يكتب الحرف الأول منها بحرف كبير)

The Nile	النيل	Amazon	نهر الأمازون
Suez Canal	قناة السويس	Mississippi	الميسيسيبي

Names of Things

<u>أسماء لأشياء مثل:</u>

car   سيارة

box   صندوق

chair   كرسي

Abstract	أسماء لمعنى أو لنعوت مثل:
	Nouns
sweetness	حلاوة
goodness	جودة – لطف – عمل كريم
generosity	سخاء – كرم – جود
whiteness	بياض – نقاء – صفاء
Collective Nouns	أسماء جمع مثل:
people (peoples – شعوب)	ناس – شعب
crew	طاقم – جماعة
group	زُمرة – مجموعة – حشْد – شرذمة

Put the following nouns

ضع الأسماء التالية في

In their proper column.

العمود الخاص بها.

The columns are numbered (1 to 4)

والخانات مرقّمة من (1إلى 4)

Gibraltar – Tripoli – team – Ahmad – Rome – desk – table – salt – The Atlas – difficulty – Sara – Nadia – cat – cow – The Alps – key – Taghreed – Everest – hungry – camel – Rabat – Amazon – Kuwait – The Nile – car – crew – cloth – Suez Canal – Mississipi – goodness – cock.

Proper Nouns (a)	Nouns Of Animals (b)	Nouns of Capitals (c)	Nouns of Mountains (d)
(1)	(1)	(1)	(1)
(2)	(2)	(2)	(2)
(3)	(3)	(3)	(3)
(4)	(4)	(4)	(4)
Names of Rivers & Canals (e)	Names of Things (f)	Abstract Nouns (g)	Collective Nouns (h)
(1)	(1)	(1)	(1)
(2)	(2)	(2)	(2)
(3)	(3)	(3)	(3)
(4)	(4)	(4)	(4)

The Articles and Plurals   أدوات النكرة والتعريف وصيغة الجمع

من الأهمية بمكان معرفة استعمال أدوات النكرة وصيغة التعريف في حالة المفرد والجمع، وهي

(a)، (an) في حالة النكرة المفردة و(the) في حـالتي التعريـف المفـرد والجمـع: وتُجمـع الأسماء في اللغـة الإنجليزية على النحو الآتي:

book – books

cat – cats

pencil - pencils

(1) بإضافة حرف (s) إلى هذه الأسماء العادية مثال:

(2) بإضافة حرفي (es) إلى الأسماء المنتهية بالحروف التالية مثل (ss) و (s) و(x) و(ch) و(sh) و(o):

class – classes, bus – buses, fox – foxes, watch- watches, bush – bushes, tomato – tomatoes.

(3) بإضافة (ies) إلى الأسماء المنتهية بحرف (y) ويكون ما قبله ساكِن مثل:

sky – skies, family – families, quantity – quantities, story – stories, city – cities.

(4) هناك أسماء تتغير بتغيُر الحرف أو الحروف المتحركة مثل:

man – men, woman – women, tooth – teeth, foot – feet, mouse – mice, ox – oxen, goose – geese.

(5) والأسماء المنتهية بحرف (f) أو (fe) تتغير إلى (ves) مثل:

knife – knives, leaf – leaves, wife – wives.

(6) هناك أسماء متشابهة في حالة المفرد والجمع مثل الأسماء التالية: متسلسل – series – series، الأيل –

الأيائل deer - deer، الخروف – الخرفان sheep - sheep، صنف – أصناف species - species، وسيلة – وسائل

means - means.

(7) هناك أسماء تُستعمل معها الأرقام (واحد اثنان وثلاثة إلخ...):

one book – three lessons – four apples – two books.

(8) وأسماء لا تُستعمل معها الأرقام مثل: water, ink, milk، ولكن إذا أُريد قليل مـن هـذه الأشياء تُوضع

كلمة (some) أمامها وتعني بعض.

الأسماء التي تقبل الأرقام ويقال عنها   (a) **Countable Nouns:**

one book – two books – three eggs – four boxes.

الأسماء التي لا تقبل معها الأرقام هي: (b) **Uncountable Nouns:**

water – milk – ink – coffee – money.

وتستعمل مع الأسماء التي لا تقبل معها الأرقام التعبيرات التالية:

كوب من الماء	(a cup of) water
كأسان من الحليب	two (glasses of) milk
أَرْبَع زجاجات من الحبر أو الماء	four (bottles of) ink/ water
كأسٌ من عصير البرتقال	a (glass of) orange juice

وإذا أردنا أن نتحدث عن أسماء ليس لها مفردات في اللغة الإنجليزية تُستعمل هذه العبـارة – (a pair of)

– وتعني (زوج من) لأي شيء ليس له مفرد مثل:

Give me (a pair of) scissors — أعطني زوجاً من المقصات

Give me (a pair of) trousers — أعطني زوجاً من السراويل

Give me (a pair of) socks — أعطني زوجاً من الجوارب

Exercise (3) Plurals — تمرين (3) (صيغة الجمع)

اجعل هذه الأسماء المختلفة (المذكورة أدناه) في حالة جمع، مضيفاً إلى الإسم حـرف (s) أو (es) أو بتغيـيره

إلى (ies) أو إلى (ves) أو ترك الاسم على ما هو مستعملاً كلمة بعض (some) للأسماء التي لا تقبل الأرقـام.

وكلمة (some) وهي أداة نكرة وتستعمل أيضاً في حالة الأسماء التي تقبل الأرقام وتأتي قبل الاسم مثل:

some books – some chairs – some people.

(a) (Plurals)

(1) airport ....

(2) article ....

(3) actor ....

(4) advice ....

(5) answer ....

(6) animal ....

(7) appointment ....…..

مطار

مقال/ بند/ مادة

ممثل مسرحي/ الفاعل

نصيحة/ إنباء

جواب/ استجابة

حيوان

موعد/ تعيين/ توظيف

(b) (Plurals)

(1) bank ....

(2) butter ....

(3) bottle ....

(4) boy ....…

(5) box ....…

(6) business ....…

(7) boundary ....…

(8) branch ....

(9) center ....

(10) chain ....

مصرف

زبدة

زجاجة/ قنينة

ولد

صندوق

مهمة/ عمل/ تجارة

حد/ تُخم

غصن

وسط/ محور

سلسلة

(11) city	مدينة
(12) cottage	كوخ
(13) century	قرن/ مئة عام
(14) date	تاريخ/ تمرة
(15) dish	صحن
(16) dictionary	قاموس
(17) dress	فستان/ ثوب
(18) knife	سكين
(19) enemy	عدو
(20) error	خطأ/ غلط
(21) examination	امتحان
(22) eye	عين
(23) employee	موظف
(24) emissary	مبعوث
(25) egoist	أناني
(26) farmer	فلاح
(27) fish	سمكة
(28) factory	مصنع
(29) family	عائلة
(30) failure	إخفاق/ تخلف
(31) girl	بنت

(32) glory ....   مجد

(33) gun ....   بندقية

(34) house ....   بيت

(35) handkerchief ....   منديل

(36) hand bag ....   حقيبة يد

(37) hospital ....   مستشفى

(38) idea ....   فكرة

(39) olive ....   زيتونة

(40) torch ....   مشعل/ بطارية

(41) video ....   مرئي

(42) utility ....   منفعة/ فائدة

(43) tip ....   بقشيش

(44) happiness ....   سعادة

(45) wolf ....   ذئب

Derivation of Nouns

اشتقاق الأسماء

Lebanon	لبنان	France	فرنسا
A Lebanese	لبناني	A French	فرنسي
The Lebanese	اللبنانيون	The French	الفرنسيون
Egypt	مصر	England	إنجلترا
An Egyptian	مصري	An English	إنجليزي
The Egyptians	المصريون	The English	الإنجليز
America	أمريكا	Russia	روسيا
An American	أميركي	A Russian	روسي
The American	الأميركان	The Russian	الروس
Japan	اليابان	Spain	إسبانيا
A Japanese	ياباني	A Spanish	اسباني
The Japanese	اليابانيون	The Spanish	الإسبان
Libya	ليبيا	China	الصين
A Libyan	ليبي	A Chinese	صيني
The Libyan	الليبيون	The Chinese	الصينيون

الضمائر الشخصية

Personal Pronouns

تستعمل الضمائر الشخصية عوضاً عن تكرار الإسم وفي حالة الفاعل فقط مثل:

(1) I ....   أنا – للمذكر والمؤنث – مفرد

(2) We ....   نحن – للمذكر والمؤنث – مثنى وجمع

(3) You ...…..........…..   أنتَ – أنتِ – مذكر ومؤنث – مفرد

(4) You ....   أنتما - للمذكر والمؤنث – مثنى جمع

(5) He ....…   هو – للمذكر – مفرد – (للغائب)

(6) They ....   هما – للمذكر والمؤنث – مثنى وجمع

(7) They ....   هم – أو هنَّ للمذكر والمؤنث – جمع

(8) She ....   هي – للمؤنث – مفرد فقط

الضمائر في حالة المفعول به

(1)	me	مذكر ومؤنث	- ني
(2)	us	مذكر ومؤنث مثنى وجمع	- نا
(3)	you	مذكر ومؤنث مفرد	كَ - كِ
(4)	you	مذكر ومؤنث مثنى وجمع	- كما
(5)	him	للغائب مذكّر	- ـه
(6)	her	للغائبة مؤنث	- ها
(7)	them	مذكر ومؤنث مثنى	- هما
(8)	them	مذكر ومؤنث جمع	- هم - هنَّ
(9)	them	للمؤنث - مثنى	- هما
(10)	them	للمؤنث جمع	- هنَّ

ملاحظة: يجب على الدَّارس أن ينتبه جيداً عند استعمال الـضمائر إذ أن هنـاك في اللغـة الإنجليزيـة ضـمير

يُستعمل لغير العاقل فقط. (هو أو هي) مثل: It.

هو كتاب – مفرد الضمير ومفرد الإسم It is a book.

هي/ كتب – جمع الضمير وجمع الإسم They are books.

وقد تَغَيَّر فعل الكينونة (is) إلى (are) وحُذفت أداة النكرة.

صيغة الملكية

تستعمل هذه الصيغة قبل الإسم للدلالة على ملكيته مثل:

(1) My father	is a teacher.	مفرد مذكر ومؤنث	والدي
(2) Your father	is a farmer.	مذكر	والدَك
(3) Your father	is a doctor.	مؤنث	والدِك
(4) Your father	is a Lebanese.	مذكر مثنى	والدكما
(5) Your father	is an Egyptian.	مؤنث مثنى	والدكما
(6) Your father	is a French.	مذكر جمع	والدكم
(7) Your father	is an Englishman.	مؤنث جمع	والدكنَّ
(8) His father	is weak.	مذكر	والده
(9) Her father	is a Chinese	مؤنث	والدها
(10) Our father	is an American	مذكر ومؤنث	والدنا
(11) Their father	is a Japanese	مذكر جمع	والدهم
(12) Their father	is a Lebanese	مؤنث جمع	والدهنَّ
(13) Its food	لغير العاقل مفرد (طعام القط أو الكلب مثلاً)		طعامه
(14) Their food	لغير العاقل جمع (طعام للقطط أو للكلاب مثلاً)		طعامهم

يلاحظ: استعمال فعل الكينونة (is) (يكون) مفرد في حالة المضارع. ويُستعمل فعل (are) في حالة الجمع مع التغييرات الإضافية لما قبله.

23

(a) Personal Pronouns.	وفيما يتعلّق بموضوع الضمائر الشخصية
(b) Objective Pronouns.	والضمائر في حالة المفعول به،
(c) Possessive Objectives.	وكذلك صفات الملكية،
(d) Possessive Pronouns.	والضمائر الملكية.

تخضع جميع هذه الضمائر لما قبلها سواء أكان إسماً أم ضميراً في حالة المفرد أم الجمع.

(d) Possessive Pronouns   ضمائر الملكية

تستعمل ضمائر الملكية هذه عِوَض عن تكرار الشيء المملوك مثل القول:

(1) I have a bicycle.	عندي دراجة
(2) It is (my) bicycle.	إنها دراجتي
(3) It is (mine).	إنها (لي) أو إنها (خاصتي) (إنها ملكي)
(4) It is (yours).	إنها لكَ أو (إنها خاصتك).

(1) في الجملة الأولى أخبرت إنه عندك (دراجة).

(2) وفي الجملة الثانية استعملت صفة الملكية (my) تأكيداً لملكية الدراجة.

(3) في الجملة الثالثة استعملت ضمير الملكية (mine) وذلك عوضاً عن تكرار اسم الدراجة.

ضمائر الشخصية Personal Pronouns	صفة الملكية Possessive Adjectives	ضمائر الملكية Possessive Pronouns		الاستعمال
I ……………..	my ……...	mine	لي	للتمكلم
we …………...	our ………..	ours	لَنا	جمع المتكلمين
you …………..	your ……...	yours	لكَ	للمخاطب مفرد مذكر
you …………..	your ……...	yours	لكِ	للمخاطب مفرد مؤنث
you …………..	your……...	yours	لكما	للمخاطب مثنى مذكر
you …………..	your ……...	yours	لكما	للمخاطب مثنى مؤنث
you …………..	your ……...	yours	لكم	للمخاطب جمع مذكر
you …………..	your ……...	yours	لكنَّ	للمخاطب جمع مؤنث
he …………...	his ………..	his	له	للغائب مذكر فقط
she …………...	her ………..	hers	لها	للغائبة مؤنث فقط
they …………..	their ……...	theirs	لهم	للغائب جمع مذكر
they ………....	their ……...	theirs	لهنَّ	للغائب جمع مؤنث

25

Exercise (4)

Put the Possessive Adjective

and the possessive Pronoun

in the blank space

تمرين 4

ضع صفة الملكية

وضمير الملكية المناسب

في المكان الفارغ مثل رقم (1)

Personal Pronouns	Possessive Adjectives	Possessive Pronouns	Objective Pronouns
(1) I	my	mine	me
(2) We			
(3) You			
(4) You			
(5) You			
(6) You			
(7) You			
(8) You			
(9) He			
(10) She			
(11) It			
(12) They			

(*) **ملاحظة:** يوجد في اللغة الإنجليزية ما يسمى بالضمير الغائب للجماد أو للحيوان في حالة المفرد أو

الجمع مثل: هو أو هي (مفرد – It)، (they) في حالة الجمع.

Lesson Four

الدرس الرابع

أسماء الإشارة

Demonstrative Pronouns

(1) تستعمل أسماء الإشارة للأشخاص أو للأشياء القريبة أو البعيدة، المفرد أو الجمع. والأسـماء التـي تستعمل للأشخاص أو الأشياء القريبة هي:

Examples:	مثال
This	هذا أو هذه (مفرد للقريب)
These	هؤلاء (جمع للقريب)
This man is a teacher.	هذا الرجل معلم
These men are teachers.	هؤلاء الرجال معلمون
This ball is mine.	هذه الكرة لي /خاصتي / ملكي
These balls are mine / ours.	هذه الكرات لي /لنا / مِلكنا

(2) أسماء الإشارة التي تستعمل للأشخاص أو الأشياء البعيدة تأتي قبل الإسم المفرد أو الجمع وهي:

Examples:	مثال
That	ذلك أو تلك (مفرد للبعيد)
Those	أولئك (جمع للبعيد)
That car is mine.	تلك السيارة لي /خاصتي / ملكي
Those cars are mine.	تلك السيارات لي /خاصتي / ملكي
Those cars are ours.	تلك السيارات لنا / خاصتنا / ملكنا
Another example:	**ومثال آخر في حالتي المفرد والجمع:**
This is a cow and that is a donkey.	هذه بقرة وذلك حمار.
This is a farmer and that is his horse.	هذا فلاح وذلك حصانه.
This is a hen and that is its egg.	هذه دجاجة وتلك بيضتها.
These are horses and those are donkeys.	هؤلاء أحصنة وأولئك حمير.
These are drivers and those are their cars.	هؤلاء سائقون وأولئك سياراتهم.
These are hens and those are their eggs.	هذه دجاجات وأولئك بيوضها.

الدرس الخامس **Lesson Five** فعل الكينونة

المضارع

Verb "to be" present tense

ملاحظة: إن الحرف الأول من الكلمة في بداية الجملة يكتب بحرف كبير (Capital Letter)، وفي هـذا الدرس سوف نستعمل بعض المفردات الضرورية:

Example			مثال:
Yes	نعم - بلى / أجل	Question	سؤال
No	لا – كلا	Answer	جواب/ جاوب
Not	لا – ليس – لم - لن	Complete	تمم / يتمم
Singular	مفرد	Masculine	مذكر
Plural	جمع	Feminine	مؤنث
Affirmative	إثبات	Give	أعطي
Interrogative	استفهام	Write	اكتب
Negative	نفي	The following	الآتي

يستعمل فعل الكينونة (am) مع الضمير (I) في صيغة المضارع.

يستعمل فعل الكينونة (is) مع الضمائر (he, she, it) في صيغة المضارع.

أما فعل الكينونة (are) فيستعمل مع الضمائر (you) في جميع حالاتها و(they, we).

29

Verb To Be (Present Tense)

فعل الكينونة في المضارع

Affirmative   إثبات

Affirmative   إثبات

Singular   مفرد مثل:

Plural   جمع مثل:

(1) I am a man

(2) We are men

(2) You are a farmer

(2) You are farmers

(3) He is Lebanese

(3) They are Lebanese

(4) She is a doctor

(4) They are doctors

(5) It is a cat

(5) They are cats

I am here – We are here هنا نحن – هنا أنا

إلى آخر الـضمائر التـي تـم شرحها في الـدروس You are there – You are there هناك أنتما أو هناك أنت
السابقة تفصيلياً.

Interrogative   استفهام

Interrogative   استفهام

Singular   في حالة المفرد

Plural   في حالة الجمع

(1) Am I a man?

(6) Are we men?

(2) Are you a farmer?

(7) Are you farmers?

(3) Is he a Lebanese?

(8) Are they Lebanese?

(4) Is she a woman?

(9) Are they women?

(5) Is it a cat?

(10) Are they cats?

Exercise (5) (V. To Be)

تمرين خاص بفعل الكينونة(5).

(a) Fill the spaces:

املأ الفراغ بالفعل المناسب:

(1) I ……….……..….…… a man

(6) We ………..…………… men

(2) You ………………… teacher

(7) You …...………..…. teachers

(3) He ……………..….. a Lebanese

(8) They ……………..… Lebanese

(4) She ………………… a nurse

(9) They …………..…….. nurses

(5) It ……………………. a cat

(10) They …………………. cats

(b) Answer the following questions:

أجب باستعمال – Yes-

(1) Is this a cat?   Yes, this is a cat.

(2) Are you a teacher? ……………………………………………

(3) Is she a nurse? ……………………………………………...

(4) Is he Lebanese? ……………………………………………

(5) Are we men? ……………………………………………

(6) Are they poor? ……………………………………...

(7) Are they strong? ……………………………………………

(8) Are you rich men? ……………………………………………

31

(c) Answer the following question using (No – Not)

تُستعمل (no) قبل الجملة للنفي وتستعمل (not) لنفي الفعل مثل:

(1) Is he a woman?   No, he is not a woman

(2) Is this a cat? ....

(3) Is that a boy? ....

(4) Are we American? ....

(5) Are you engineers? ....

(6) Are they housekeepers? ....

(7) Is this a pencil? ....

فعلLesson Six   الدرس السادس

الكينونة الماضي

Verb "to be" past tense

Verb To Be (Past Tense)		فعل الكينونة في زمن الماضي

Interrogative   استفهام   Interrogative   استفهام

Singular   في حالة المفرد   **Plural**   في حالة الجمع

(1) Was I a boy?   (6) Were we boys?

(2) Were you a farmer?   (7) Were you farmers?

(3) Was he a rich man?   (8) Were they rich men?

(4) Was she a girl?   (9) Were they girls?

(5) Was it a dog?   (10) Were they dogs?

Exercise (6):   تمرين خاص بفعل الكينونة الماضي(6):

(a) Fill in the missing verb (Past Tense):   (أ) املأ الفراغات بالفعل المناسب

(1) I .... a boy.   (6) We .... boys.

(2) You .... a farmer.   (7) You .... farmers.

(3) He .... rich man.   (8) They .... rich men.

(4) She .... girl.   (9) They .... girls.

(5) It .... a dog.   (10) They .... dogs.

(b) Answer the following questions:

أجب باستعمال – Yes -

(1) Was this a cat?   Yes, this was a cat.

(2) Were you a doctor? ....

(3) Was she a girl? ....

(4) Was he Syrian? ....

(5) Were we doctors? ....

(6) Were they poor? ....

(7) Were they strong? ....

(8) Were they rich men? ....

(c) Answer the following questions using (No/not)

(1) Was this a cat?   No, this was not a cat.

(2) Were you a doctor? ....

(3) Was she a girl? ....

(4) Was he Syrian? ....

(5) Were we doctors? ....

(6) Were they poor? ....

(7) Were they strong? ....

(8) Were they rich men? ....

Summary of verb To Be

خلاصة فعل الكينونة

Singular مفرد	Plural جمع	Singular مفرد	Plural جمع
Affirmative	**Affirmative**	**Interrogative**	**Interrogative**
(1) I am …….	We are ……	(1) Am I ……..?	Are we …….?
(2) You are ….	You are …..	(2) Are you ….?	Are you ……?
(3) He is ……..	They are ….	(3) Is he ………?	Are they ……?
(4) She is …….	They are ….	(4) Is she …..…?	Are they ……?
(5) It is ……….	They are ….	(5) Is it ………?	Are they ……?
(6) I was ……..	Were we ….	(6) Was I …….?	Were we …..?
(7) You were….	You were ….	(7) Were you…?	Were you ….?
(8) He was ……	They were….	(8) Was he …..?	Were they….?
(9) She was …..	They were ….	(9) Was she ….?	Were they …?
(10) It was ……	They were …..	(10) Was it …..?	Were they …?

المستقبل

Verb "to be" future tense

يستعمل هذا الفعل لأجل أي حدث في المستقبل (shall) أو (will). وهذا الفعل (shall أو هذا الفعل

will) والذي يعني أو يقابله (سوف) في اللغة العربية وهو من مجموعة الأفعال المساعدة بمعنى أنه يمكن

أن يتكون منه السؤال والنفي دون الحاجة إلى فعل آخر لهذا الإجراء اللغوي. ومصدر الفعل (The

infinitive) يُبيّن شكل الفعل دون تحديد الزمن ويَسبقه دائماً حرف (to) في حالة المضارع. فعل يملك to

have ويتفرع منه has – have وفعل يجيء to come فعل يكتب

– to write – وفعل يرى - to see.

وللتعبير عن المستقبل يستعمل (will – shall) يليها فعل الكينونة (be) وكما تستعمل (shall) مع

الضمائر (I, we)، أما (will) فتستعمل مع باقي الضمائر.

| (a) Verb To be | فعل الكينونة | (b) Verb To Be | فعل الكينونة في |
| Present Tense | في المضارع | Future Tense | زمن المستقبل |

(1) I am a boy[1].	(1) I shall be a man.
(2) You are a soldier.	(2) You will be an officer.
(3) He is a student.	(3) He will be a doctor.
(4) She is a girl.	(4) She will be a woman.
(5) It is a kitten.	(5) It will be a cat.
(6) We are boys.	(6) We shall be men.
(7) You are soldiers.	(7) You will be officers.
(8) They are students.	(8) They will be doctors.

ملاحظة: يستعمل (will) للتعبير عن الإرادة مثل:

I will write the letter today. (تأكيداً) سأكتب الرسالة اليوم

| (a) Interrogative | استفهام | (b) Affirmative | إثبات في |
| | في زمن المستقبل | | زمن المستقبل |

Future Tense	Future Tense
(1) Shall I be a man?	Yes, I shall be a man.
(2) Will you be an officer?	Yes, I shall be an officer.
(3) Will he be a teacher?	Yes, he will be a teacher.
(4) Will she be a woman?	Yes, she will be a woman.
(5) Will it be a cat?	Yes, it will be a cat.

---

[1] - وفيما يلي اختصار لفعل الكينونة في حالة المضارع في حالة إثبات ونفي وفي المحادثة.
(1) I'm – you're – he's – She's – It's – We're – You're – They're.
(2) I'm not – You're not – He isn't – She isn't – It isn't – They aren't.

| (6) Shall we be officers? | Yes, we shall be officers. |
| (7) Will they be teachers? | Yes, they will be teachers. |

(a) Negative Future Tense	**(b) Negative Future Tense**
نفي في زمن المستقبل	نفي في زمن المستقبل
(1) No, I shall not be a man.	No, you will not be a farmer.
(2) No, you will not be an officer.	No, we shall not be officers.
(3) No, he will not be a teacher.	No, they will not be teachers.
(4) No, she will not be a woman.	No, you will not be a farmer.

كما يمكن اختصار (shall, will) على الشكل التالي:

(1) (I'll) be a man.	I'll be	ويلفظ أَلْ بي
(2) (You'll) be a teacher.	You'll be	ويلفظ يُولْ بي
(3) (He'll) be an officer.	He'll be	ويلفظ هِيلْ بي
(4) (She'll) be a woman.	She'll be	ويلفظ شيل بي
(5) (We'll) be men.	We'll be	ويلفظ وِيْلْ بي
(6) (They'll) be teachers.	They'll be	ويلفظ ذايْل بي

ملاحظة: مكانة الفاصلة العليا وهي تأتي ما بين الضمير والفعل في الاختصار.

Vocabulary		المفردات التي تُستعمل مع فعل المستقبل:	
Tomorrow	غداً	Next month	الشهر المقبل
Next time	في المرة التالية	In future	مستقبلاً
Every day	كل يوم	One day	يوماً ما
Again	من جديد/مرة ثانية	On Monday	يوم الاثنين
Next week	الأسبوع المقبل	At seven o'clock	عند الساعة السابعة.
		Now	الآن – وتـــستعمل مـــع
			المضارع

أمثلة:

1- I'll be a doctor next month.

2- He'll be here on Monday.

3- She'll go to Beirut Tomorrow.

4- They'll climb the hell again on Tuesday.

(a) Interrogative in the future	(b) Negative in the future
جُمل في حالة السؤال	جُمل في حالة النفي
في زمن المستقبل	في زمن المستقبل
(1) Will I be a farmer?	I won't be a farmer.
(2) Will you be a teacher?	You won't be a teacher.
(3) Will he have a car?	He won't have a car.
(4) Will she have a ball?	She won't have a ball.

(5) Will it have its food?   It won't have its food.

(6) Will we have our farm?   We won't have our farm.

(7) Will they have bicycles?   They won't have bicycles.

ملاحظة: إن التعبير(I won't be a farmer) في حالة النفي هـو الاختـصار للجملـة (**I will not be a**
farmer). كما أن هذا الفعل في حالته المختصرة يُستعمل في السؤال المنفي ويلفظ – (وُونْتْ)won't.

وهناك استعمال آخر لكلمة (will) في التعبيرات التالية:

For wish: (1) للتعبير عن (التمني والرغبة مثل:

I will go if you do.   سوف أذهب إذا أردت (أنتَ)

For desire: (2) للتعبير عن الرغبة مثل:

We cannot always do as we will.   لا يمكننا دائماً أن نفعل مثل ما نرغب.

For will: (3) للتعبير عن الإرادة مثل:

To learn one must have a strong will.   للتعلم يجب أن يكون للمرء أو للفرد إرادة قوية.

بينما كلمة (Shall) التي صارت نادرة الاستعمال في زمن المستقبل في هذه الأيام في اللغة الإنجليزية فإن لها

استعمالات أخرى مثلاً:

Shall:

(1) للتعبير عن أمر ما – أو وجوب ما مثل:

You shall go to the party, I

(أنت) ســوف تــذهب إلى / أو يجــب أن تــذهب إلى الحفلة، أعِدُك.

promise you.

(2) للتعبير عن تعهد / إلزام المرء نفسه بــأداء عمــل مــا مثل:

He shall drink his milk even if I have to

(هو) سوف يشرب أو هو ملزم أن يشرب الحليب، حتى لو أُجبرتُ على صبه في حلقه.

pour it down his throat.

Necessity:

(للتعبير عن الضرورة مثل:)

He shall go to school.

(هو) يجب أن يذهب إلى المدرسة

ملاحظة: يستعمل الفاعل في اللغة الإنجليزية بعكس اللغة العربية التي تبدأ بالفعل.

Exercise (7):

(a) Change the following

Sentences into the future tense:

1- I go to school everyday ……………………………………..

2- We have lunch in your house ……………………………….

3- They are students now. ……………………………………

4- We are very happy ……………………………………….

5- I have a new bicycle ……………………………………...

6- We are here today ……………………………………….

7- They have knives ………………………………………...

8- It has its food ………………………………………….

9- I am tired ……………………………………………

10- They were there today ……………………………………

(b) Write down the short

form of (will not)

أكتب الاختصار

لشكل (will not) في هذا الفراغ.

1- I will be a farmer ………………………………………

2- You will be a teacher ……………………………………

3- He will have a ball ………………………………………

4- She will have a car ………………………………………

5- We will have our farm …………………………………....

6- They will have their bicycles …………………………………

Lesson Eight

فعل الملكية في حالة الحاضر

Verb "To Have" present tense

فعل ملك / عند / حاز

في حالة المضارع

Verb To Have

Present Tense

سؤال   (b) Interrogative   إثبات   **(a) Affirmative**

1- Have I a car?	1- I have a car.
2- Have we cars?	2- We have cars.
3- Has he a pen?	3- He has a pen.
4- Has she a cat?	4- She has a cat.
5- Has it its food?	5- It has its food.
6- Have you houses?	6- You have houses.
7- Have they farmers?	7- They have farmers.

جمل في حالة نفي: **(c) Negative Sentences:**

1- I have not a car.

2- We have not cars.

3- He has not a pen.

4- She has not a cat.

5- It has not its food.

6- You have not houses.

7- They have not farmers.

(d) Vocabulary:	مفردات جديدة (كل هذه الأسماء تجمع بحرف (s) أو (es):
picture	صورة
notebook	دفتر / مذكرة
map	خريطة
newspaper	صحيفة/ جريدة
door	باب
room	حجرة
window	نافذة
language	لغة
club	نادي
station	محطة
train	قطار
cup	فنجان
table	منضدة / طاولة
line	خط
magazine	مجلة
necktie	ربطة عنق
bus	حافلة / باص
telegram	برقية
telephone	هاتف

Lesson Nine

الدرس التاسع

فعل الملكية في حالة الماضي

Verb "to have" past tense

Verb To Have		فعل يملك أو عنده
Past Tense		في حالة الماضي (كان يملك)

(a) Affirmative	إثبات	(b) Interrogative	سؤال
1- I had a picture.		Had I a picture?	
2- We had pictures.		Had we pictures?	
3- He had a map.		Had he a map?	
4- She had a magazine.		Had she a magazine?	
5- It had its food.		Had it its food?	
6- You had a telegram.		Had you a telegram?	
7- They had a newspaper.		Had they a news paper?	

(c) Negative:	جمل في حالة نفي:

1- I had not a picture.

2- We had not pictures.

3- He had not a map.

4- She had not a magazine.

5- It had not its food.

6- You had not a telephone.

7- They had not a newspaper.

وفي ما يلي تصريف فعل (had) باللغة العربية.

ملاحظة: أن هذا الفعل المساعد في حالة الماضي لم يتغيّر مع جميع الضمائر ويبقى كما هو في حالة الإثبات والسؤال والنفي كذلك. والأفعال هي: (كان عندي – كان عندنا – كان عنده – كان عندها – كان عنده أو عندها لغير العاقل – كان عندك أو عندكم أو عندكنّ وكان عندهم أو عندهنّ.

Exercise (8):	تمرين (8):
(a) Change the following	حوّل الجمل الآتية الإخبارية
Statements into questions:	إلى سؤال مثل:

1- I have a house.   Have I a house?

2- We have a picture ....?

3- He has a pencil ....?

4- She has a copybook ....?

5- It has its food ....?

6- You have pens ....?

7- They have newspapers ....?

(b) Change the following

Statements into negative:

1- I have a picture.   I have not a picture.

2- We have a house …………………………………

3- He has a room …………………………………

4- She has a dress …………………………………...

5- It has a ball …………………………………

6- You have a magazine …………………………………

7- They have their map …………………………………...

ملاحظة: أن اختصار فعل (يملك) في المضارع وفي الماضي (كان يملك)، يكون على الوجه الآتي في حالة السؤال

المنفي وفي المحادثة فقط مثل:

1- Haven't I a picture?   ألّا أملك صورة؟ أو ليس عندي صورة؟

2- Haven't we a house?   ألا نملك بيتاً؟ أو ليس عندنا بيتاً؟

3- Hasn't he a paper?   ألا يملك ورقة؟ أو ليس عنده ورقة؟

4- Hasn't she a magazine?   ألا تملك مجلة؟ أليس لها مجلة؟

5- Hasn't it a doll?   ألا يملك أو تملك (لغير العاقل) دمية؟

6- Haven't you a pencil?   ألَا تملك قلم رصاص؟ أو لا تملكون قلم رصاص؟

7- Haven't they their telephone?   ألا يملكون هاتفهم؟

وفيما يلي اختصار فعل يملك (كان يملك في الماضي) وفي المحادثة فقط:

1- Hadn't I a car?	ألم يكن لي أو عندي سيارة؟
2- Hadn't we a house?	ألم يكن لنا أو عندنا بيتاً؟
3- Hadn't he a ball?	ألم يكن له أو عنده كرة؟
4- Hadn't she a magazine?	ألم يكن لها أو عندها مجلة؟
5- Hadn't she a ball?	ألم تكن أو تكن لها كرة؟
6- Hadn't you a map?	ألم يكن لك أو عندك خريطة؟
7- Hadn't they their book?	ألم يكن لهم أو لهنَّ كتاب؟

(c) Answer the above mentioned

questions negatively:

1- I hadn't a car.

2- ....

3- ....

4- ....

5- ....

6- ....

7- ....

أجب عن الأسئلة

المذكورة أعلاه بالنفي مثل:

Lesson Ten

الدرس العاشر

فعل الملكية في حالة المستقبل

Verb "to have" future tense

Verb To Have in the Future Tense

فعل يملك في زمن المستقبل:

(a) Affirmative

1- I shall have a picture.

2- We shall have our house.

3- You will have your map.

4- He will have a paper.

5- She will have a magazine.

6- It will have its food.

7- You will have your bicycles.

8- They will have their books.

(b) Interrogative

Shall I have a picture?

Shall we have our house?

Will you have your map?

Will he have a paper?

Will she have a magazine?

Will it have its food?

Will you have your bicycles?

Will they have their books?

(c) Negative:

جمل في حالة نفي:

1- I shall not have a picture tomorrow.

2- We shall not have our house in future.

3- You will not have your paper today.

4- He will not have his map next week.

5- She will not have her magazine today.

6- It will not have its food tomorrow.

7- They will not have their books next month.

1- I shan't have a picture tomorrow.

2- We shan't have our house in future.

3- You won't have your paper today.

4- He won't have his map next week.

5- She won't have her magazine today.

6- It won't have its food tomorrow.

7- They won't have their books next month.

زمن المضارع البسيط

Simple Present Tense

(1) يستعمل المضارع البسيط في الأعمال التي تحدثُ أو تقعُ يومياً – كعادة أو أسلوب منتظم في الذهاب إلى الإدارة أو في قراءة الصحف. وكذلك في بعض الأوقات أو مرة في الأسبوع أو في الشهر. وكذلك عادة المرء يومياً في غسل الوجه وفي تنظيف الأسنان وفي تناول الفطور وفي مصاحبة الأولاد إلى المدرسة وغيرها من الأعمال العادية الروتينية. ولنأخذ مثلاً:

فعل (To go) (يذهب) كمثال في شرح هذه الصيغة الزمنية:

(2) تظهر الأفعال الإنجليزية في غير القواميس وقبلها حرف (To) مثل: To see – To write – To talk To sleep – – لتدل على المصدر أو صيغة المصدر (The Stem) إلا أن حرف (To) يحـذف عنـد استعمال الفعل في الجملة مثل: I go– I see – I write – I talk – I buy

(3) يُضاف إلى الأفعال في زمن المضارع البسيط وللضمير الغائب الآتي: حرف (s) أو (es) أو بتغير حرف (y) للفعل المنتهي بهذا الحرف إلى (i) ويضاف إليه (es). ولكن إذا انتهى الفعل بحـرف (y) ومـا قبلـه حـرف متحرك يضاف إليه (s) فقط مثل: (يلعب) He plays.

Examples:	أمثلة:	أمثلة للشروح المذكورة أعلاه
(a) Verb to see	فعل يرى	حرف (to) قبل الفعل يحذف عند استعمال الفعل
(1) He sees	(هو) يرى	أضيف حرف (s) لأن الفعل منتهي بـ (e)
(2) She sees	(هي) ترى	أضيف حرف (s) لأن الفعل منتهي بـ (e)
(3) It sees	(هو أو هي) ترى	أضيف حرف (s) لأن الفعل منتهي بـ (e)
(b) Verb to teach	فعل يُعَلِّم	حرف (to) قبل الفعل يحذف عند استعمال الفعل
(1) He teaches	(هو) يُعَلِّم	أضيف حرف (es) لأن الفعل منتهي بـ (ch)
(2) She teaches	(هي) تُعَلِّم	أضيف حرف (es) لأن الفعل منتهي بـ (ch)
(a) To study	فعل يدرس	حرف (to) قبل الفعل ليبيّن مصدره قبل الاستعمال
(1) He studies	(هو) يدرس	تمّ تغيير حرف (y) إلى حرف (i) وأضيف إليه (es)
(2) She studies	(هي) تدرس	تمّ تغيير حرف (y) إلى حرف (i) وأضيف إليه (es)
(b) To fly	(فعل) يطير	حرف (to) قبل الفعل ليبيّن مصدره قبل الاستعمال.
(1) He flies	(هو) يطير	تمّ تغيير حرف(y) إلى حرف (i) وأضيف إليه (es)
(2) She flies	(هي) تطير	تمّ تغيير حرف (y) إلى حرف (i) وأضيف إليه (es)
(3) It flies	(هو/هي) تطير	تمّ تغيير حرف (y) إلى حرف (i) وأضيف إليه (es)

ولكن لاحظ أن الفعل المنتهي بحرف (y) وما قبله حرف متحرك بمثل فعل (to play) (يلعب)

يضاف إليه (s) فقط للضمير الغائب. بينما في بقية الضمائر:

(I – we – you - they) لا يضاف إلى الفعل حرف (s) مثال ذلك:

Example:

(1) I study	I go	I play
(2) He studies	He goes	He plays
(3) She studies	She goes	It plays
(4) It studies	It goes	It plays
(5) We study	We go	We play
(6) You study	You go	You play
(7) They study	They go	They play

(4) وهناك مفردات وكلمات تُستعمل قبل أو بعد الفعل المراد استعماله في حالة زمن المضارع

البسيط: Simple Present Tense:

والكلمات التي تستعمل قبل الفعل هي الآتي:

everyday	كل يوم
sometimes	بعض الوقت / أحياناً / من حين إلى آخر
often (ofen)	كثيراً ما / في أحوال كثيرة وتنطق (أوفن)
always	دائماً / أبداً (ظرف حال)
never	أبداً / قط (ظرف حال)
usually (يوجوالي)	عادة / من المألوف (ظرف حال) وتنطق
regularly	على نحو نظامي / منتظم (ظرف حال)

وتأتي هذه المفردات الظرفية قبل الفعل مثال ذلك:

Example:

1- I sometimes go to see my friend Ali in his house.

2- I always go to see my friend Ali in his house.

3- I never go to see my friend Ali in his house.

4- I usually go to see my friend Ali in his house.

5- I regularly go to see my friend Ali in his house.

وتستعمل الكلمات الظرفية التالية في نهاية الجملة:

Late	متأخر / متأخراً	once a day	مرة واحدة في اليوم
at midnight	عند منتصف الليل	twice a month	مرتين في الشهر
Early	مبكراً	once a week	مرة في الأسبوع
twice a day	مرتين في اليوم	during summer	أثناء الصيف
during winter	أثناء الشتاء	everyday	كل يوم
once more	مرة أُخرى	at once	في الحال
on time	في الميعاد	then	حينئذ / ثمّ

New words			مفردات جديدة
hair dresser			مزين شعر النساء
Barber			حلاق
at home			في المنزل
got out (went out)			يخرج / خرج
time (in time)			وقت / زمن (في الوقت المناسب)

تستعمل هذه الكلمات الظرفية في الزمن المضارع البسيط بعد الفعل وهي الآتي:

1- I go to sleep at midnight.

2- He goes to sleep at nine o'clock.

3- She goes to the hairdresser twice a week.

4- The dog goes to the garden everyday.

5- We write our letters every two weeks.

6- You get your newspapers everyday.

7- They sit at home during winter time.

8- They go out home during summer time.

Exercise on verbs:
                                                   تمرين على الأفعال:

نذكر أن حرف (to) الذي يأتي قبل الفعل والذي يبيّن أن الفعل لم يوضع في الزمن المحدد لـه، يُحـذف عنـد

استعماله في تركيب الجملة:

To smoke	يُدَخِّن	To tell	يُخْبر / يحكي
To swim	يعوم	To run	يجري/يدير/يُسير
To get	ينال / يتلقى	To carry	يحمل/ينقل/يقود
To come	يأتي/يجري/يصل إلى	To teach	يُعَلِّم/يُدَرِّس/يُلَقِّن
To want	يريد/يرغب/يتوق	To eat	يأكل
To hear	يسمع	To speak	يتكلم
To know	يعرف/يعلم	To try	يحاول/يُجَرِّب
To wish	يريد/يبتغي/يرغب	To ride	يركب/يمتطي
To drive	يقود/يسوق	To fight	يتقاتل/يناضل
To do	يعمل/يفعل/يبذل	To live	يعيش/يسكن
To sell	يبيع	To say	يقول/يزعم/يلفظ

Exercise (9): تمرين (9):

(a) Correct These Verbs In The Brackets:

صحح هذه الأفعال الموضوعة بين القوسين في الصيغة المناسبة:

1- The train (to go) slowly.

2- He (to play) the ball well.

3- The boy (to run) in the garden.

4- They (to live) in that house.

5- Amira (to come) home early everyday.

6- Naima (to study) English in her room.

7- He (to eat) his breakfast in his room.

8- Ali (to write) his book in his class.

9- The student (to study) his lesson well.

10- She (to help) her mother in the kitchen.

11- He (to do) his exercise at home.

12- My tooth (to hurt) me badly.

13- Mustafa (to take) his bicycle everyday.

14- The cat (to swim) in the pool.

15- He (to drive) his car to the market.

16- She always (to understand) her lesson easily.

17- We generally (to read) our paper in the house.

18- In the morning he (to wake) at 8 o'clock.

19- He always (to clean) his teeth before breakfast.

20- Layla sometimes (to speak) English with me.

ملاحظة: لكي نحوّل من الجملة الثابتة (affirmative) في زمن المضارع البسيط، إلى نفي نستعمل معها فعل (do) وnot أي (do not) واختصاره(don't) قبل الفعل للضمائر (I – we – you – they) وأما بقية الضمائر (he – she – it) يُستعمل لنفي الجملة فعل (does) وnot (does not) أي واختصاره (doesn't) في المحادثة مع حذف حرف (s) أو (es) من الفعل المستعمل مع الضمير الغائب:

(1) Affirmative إثبات	(2) Negative نفي
(1) I go to sleep early.	I do not go to sleep early.
(2) We go to sleep late.	We do not go to sleep late.
(3) You get your newspaper.	You do not get your newspaper.
(4) They sit at home.	They do not sit at home.
(5) They write their lesson.	They do not write their lesson.
(6) He studies his lesson.	He does not study his lesson
(7) She plays with the ball.	She does not play with the ball.
(8) It eats its food.	It does not eat its food.

ولكي نجعل الجملة الثابتة في الرقم (1) في حالة سؤال Interrogative نستعمل (do) مع الضمائر (we – I

he – she -it) (does)و (– you - they) مع الضمائر (مثال ذلك:

Example:

(1) I go to sleep at night.	Do I go to sleep at night?
(2) We go to school everyday.	Do we go to school everyday?
(3) You get your newspaper everyday.	Do you get your newspaper everyday?
(4) They sit at home everyday.	Do they sit at home everyday?
(5) He studies his lesson everyday	Does he study his lesson everyday?
(6) She plays with the ball everyday.	Does she play with the ball everyday?
(7) It eats its food everyday.	Does it eat its food everyday?

ملاحظة: فعل (do وdoes) وهما من الأفعال المساعدة.

(B) Make these sentences negative:

إجعل الجمـل التاليـة في حالـة نفـي. وتـذكّر أن فعـل(do not) وفعـل (does not) الأول للجمـع والثاني للمفرد وموقعهما بين الإسم أو الضمير والفعل:

Affirmative   **Negative**

1- I play football every week.

2- We write our letters at home.

3- He knows his name very well.

4- She sells apples everyday.

5- He wishes to go to London.

6- It plays with its ball.

Lesson Twelve   الدرس الثاني عشر

زمن الماضي البسيط

Simple Past Tense

للتعبير عـن فعـل حـدث في زمـن المـاضي، يُستعمل المـاضي البـسيط ويضاف إلى الفعـل المـراد

استعماله حرف (d) أو (ed) أو (t). وتُسمى الأفعال التي يضاف إليها هذه الحروف، أفعال قياسية:

Regular verbs in the

الأفعال القياسية في زمن الماضي:

Present Simple Tense:		Past Simple Tense	
To walk	يسير / يمشي	walked	سار
To help	يساعد	helped	ساعد
To wait	ينتظر	waited	انتظر
To pay	يدفع	paid	دفع
To learn	يتعلم	learned	تعلم
To mean	يعني / يقصد	meant	عنى / قصد
To hope	يأمل	hoped	أمل
To like	يلائم/يحب/يرغب	liked	لام / حب / رغب
To laugh	يضحك	laughed	ضحك
To kiss	يقبّل	kissed	قبّل
To finish	يكمل	finished	كمّل/تمم/أنهى

61

To clean	يُنَظِّف	cleaned	نظف
To hear	يسمع/يصغي	heard	سمع/أصغى
To live	يعيش/يسكن	lived	عاش/سكن
To study	يدرس	studied	درس
To wish	يرغب/يتمنى	wished	رغب/تمنى
To smoke	يُدَخِّن	smoked	دَخَّن

Irregular Verbs

وبعد أن عرفنا ما هي الأفعال القياسية (regular verbs) والتي يضاف إلها حرف (d) أو(ed)

أو(t)، نأتي إلى نوع آخر من الأفعال غير القياسية (irregular verbs) التي لا يُضاف إليها أي حرف بل

تتغير الأفعال بواسطة الحروف المتحركة(The vowels). وفيما يلي بعض منها على أن هـذه الأفعـال يجـب

حفظها عن ظهر قلب:

Present Simple Tense:		Past Simple Tense	
Irregular Verbs	أفعال شاذة	Irregular Verbs	أفعال شاذة
do – does	يفعل/يعمل	did	فعل/عمل
is	يكون (مفرد)	was	كان (مفرد)
are	يكون (جمع)	were	كان (جمع)
go	يذهب	went	ذهب
come	يأتي/يجيء	came	جاء/أتى
get	يتحصّل	got	تحصّل
drive	يقود	drove	قاد

tell	يخبر	told	أخبر
leave	يترك	left	ترك
teach	يعلِّم	taught	علَّم
eat	يأكل	ate	أكل
write	يكتب	wrote	كتب
take	يأخذ	took	أخذ
read	يقرأ	read	قرأ
speak	يتكلَّم	spoke	تكلَّم
know	يعرف/يعلم	knew	عرف/علم

تُستعمل هذه الكلمات التالية في زمن الماضي البسيط مثل:

1- ago (long ago)	منذ / منذ مدة
2- last year	السنة الماضية
3- last night	الليلة الماضية
4- last summer	الصيف الماضي
5- last winter	الشتاء الماضي
6- last month	الشهر الماضي
7- last week	الأسبوع الماضي
8- two days ago	منذ يومين / في اليومين الماضيين
9- today (اليوم)	أمس (yesterday)
10- this afternoon	اليوم بعد الظهر (بعد الظهر)
11- this evening	في هذا المساء (الليلة)

لتحويل الجمل الثابتة (Affirmative) إلى جملة منفية في الماضي (Negative) نستعمل أو نستعين بالفعل

(did not) (لم) واختصاره (didn't) لجميع الضمائر دون استثناء مثل:

He spoke English well – He didn't speak English well.

I – We – You – She – It – They – (did not ....)

ولكن لاحظ أن الفعل المراد نفيه والذي يأتي بعد (did not) يجب في هـذه الحالـة أن يكـون في المـضارع البسيط.

Exercise (10):	تمرين (10):

(a) Make these sentences negative:

اجعل الجمل الآتية في حالة نفي:

(a) Affirmative	إثبات	Negative	نفي:
1- I (went) to sleep early[1].		1-	
2- He (came) home soon[2].		2-	
3- She (went) to her home.		3-	
4- The dog (ate) its food.		4-	
5- We (wrote) our letters.		5-	
6- They (sat) at home.		6-	
7- They (went) out last night.		7-	
8- Ali (read) his lesson.		8-	
9- He (told) his story well.		9-	
10- They (got) their money.		10-	

---

1 - early = مبكراً.
2 - soon = باكراً – سريعاً لاحظ أن فعل (did not) يعني (لم) أداة نفي في اللغة العربية.

11- Layla studied her lesson. 11- ....

12- She played with the ball. 12- ....

13- I hoped to come today. 13- ....

14- She took her bicycle. 14- ....

(b) Make these sentences interrogative: حول هذه الجمل إلى سؤال

والطريقة لتحويل الجملة الثابتة (Affirmative) إلى سؤال (Interrogative) نضع الفعل (did) في حـرف
كبير (Did) (هل) أمام الجملة المراد تحويلها إل سؤال عـلى أنـه يجـب مراعـاة القاعـدة ألا وهـي تحويـل
الفعل في الجملة الثابتة إلى زمن المضارع البسيط. مثل:

He spoke English well. Did he speak English well.

(b) Affirmative إثبات **Interrogative:** :السؤال

1- I (went) to sleep early[1]. 1- ....

2- He finished his lesson. 2- ....

3- She liked her ball. 3- ....

4- The dog ate its food. 4- ....

5- We waited for him here. 5- ....

6- They learned the way. 6- ....

7- You laughed at him. 7- ....

8- They went out last night. 8- ....

9- He told his story well. 9- ....

10- They got their money. 10- ....

---

¹ early = مبكراً.

11- Layla studied her lesson.   11- …………………………..

12- She played with the ball.   12- …………………………..

13- I hoped to come today.   13- …………………………..

14- She took her bicycle.   14- …………………………..

ملاحظة: إن فعل (did) في السؤال يعني (هل) في اللغة العربية في زمن الماضي.

66

1- I (to go) to sleep last night.

2- He (to come) home at eight o'clock.

3- She (to go) to the market last week.

4- The dog (to eat) its food this morning.

5- we (to write) our letters two days ago.

6- They (to sit) at home yesterday.

7- They (to go) out last winter.

8- Sami and Mazen (to read) their lessons today.

9- He (to tell) his story to the officer this evening.

10- The train (to run) last month to Rome.

11- I (to play) football this afternoon.

12- We (to write) our letters at home last night.

13- He (to know) his lesson very well last summer.

14- She (to wish) to go to London last winter.

15- He (to pay) his account last year.

16- They (to take) him from home last night.

17- They (to study) their story well last week.

18- Layla (to drive) her bicycle well this spring.

Lesson Thirteen

الدرس الثالث عشر

المبتدأ والخبر

Subject and Object

تتكون الجملة الإخبارية غير المنفية على النحو الآتي:

(1) من اسم أو ضمير ويطلق عليه The subject أي الفاعل أو المبتـدأ – – I – Yousef – Ail
(The subject) we – he.

(2) من فعل واحد مثل (go) أو من فعلين مثـل (shall go) أو أكـثر مـن فعـل مثـل: (have I
been writing) my letter.

(3) من اسم شيء مثل: (house – orange - bicycle) إلخ. She has an – I have a bicycle
orange. ويطلق على كلمة (orange) و(bicycle) وكذلك (the house) (object) أي المفعول بـه ويمكـن
أن يكون أحياناً هذا المفعول في شكل نعت مثل (bad) أو ظرف مثـل (quickly) بـسرعة أو (yesterday)
أمس أو (here) أو في شبه جملة خالية من الفعل. وتعني (phrase) شبه جملة the cat/ is playing/ in
the garden.

الفاعل	الفعل	المفعول به
Subject	Verb	Object
I	shall go	home
We always	go	to school everyday.
The train	stops	at Paris.
That woman	makes	bread.
She often	cuts the bread	with her knife
They	will go	to France
He	wants	some juice.
We	are coming	to your house.

زمن المضارع المستمر

Present Continuous Tense

يستعمل «زمن المضارع المستمر» للتعبير عن حدث أو عمل قد بدأ وما زال مستمراً ولم ينتهي بعد.

ويتكون زمن المضارع المستمر present continuous tense مـن فعـل الكينونـة verb to be

على النحو الآتي:

أولاً: استعمال فعل الكينونة (am – is - are):

ثانياً: الفعل المراد استعماله لنأخذ مثلاً فعل: study وwrite

ثالثاً: يُضاف إلى الفعل المستعمل مقطع مكون من ثلاث حـروف (ing) وهنـاك بعـض الكلـمات

المستعملة في زمن المضارع المستمر وهي:

now   الآن/ في الوقت الحاضر/ توّاً

at this moment   في هذه اللحظة

Examples: مثل:

I am writing this lesson now.   أنا أكتب هذا الدرس الآن

He is studying this tense now.   هو يدرس هذا الزمن الآن

ملاحظة: قد استعمل الضميران قبل فعل (am) و(is) ثم استعمل الفعل (write) وأُضيف المقطع (ing) مـع

حذف حرف (e) من الفعل. واستعمل في المثل الثاني

الفعل (study) وأُضيف إليه المقطع (ing) دون أن يتغير الحرف الأخير (y) لأن هناك حرف ساكن في نهاية الفعل الأصلي. كما أنه لا يستعمل في اللغة الإنجليزية عدداً من الأفعال في زمن المضارع ولا في زمن الماضي المستمرين إلا نادراً وفي أحداث ضيقة جداً. مثل تقول: I want - ولا تقول I am wanting وكذلك تقول: I wish - ولا تقول I am wishing.

وفيما يلي جدول الأفعال وعددها 24 والتي تستعمل في حالات نادرة:

believe	يصدق	forgive	يصفح/يغفر	notice	يعلن
care	يهتم بـ	hear	يسمع	own	يملك
consist	يتألف من	hate	يحقد/يكره	possess	يقتني
contain	يحتوي	know	يعرف	refuse	يرفض
desire	يرغب	like	يحب/يود	remember	يتذكر
feel	يشعر	love	يعشق	see	يرى
forget	ينسى	matter	يهم	seem	يبدو

ولكن هذا لا يمنع من استعمال الأفعال المذكورة أعلاه في غير زمن الاستمرار وذلك فقط في المضارع البسيط والماضي البسيط وفي المستقبل.

Exercise (12):

Put the verbs in brackets

in the Present

Simple Tense or in the

Present Continuous Tense

تمرين (12):

ضع الأفعال بين القوسين

في زمن المضارع البسيط

أو في زمن المضارع المستمر

حسب وضع الجملة

1- He always (to go) to the school on foot.

2- I (to finish) my work now.

3- She (to learn) Arabic every morning.

4- They (to go out) at the present time.

5- We (to tell) our story now.

6- Ali (to play) music every week.

7- Layla (to study) English now.

8- Ali and Yousef (to take) their bicycle every month.

9- He (to come) to work very soon.

Present Continuous Tense.

زمن المضارع المستمر.

بصيغة هذا السؤال يستطيع الدَّارس أن يفهم جيداً ما المقصود بزمن المضارع المستمر. كما أن

بعض النحويين يطلق عليه بالإنجليزي Present Progressive Tense والسؤال الذي يطرح بالنسبة لهذه

الصيغة:

What are you doing now?

ماذا تفعل الآن؟

I am writing my lesson now.

الجواب: أنا أكتب درسي الآن.

New Verbs		أفعال جديدة		أفعال جديدة	
To repair	يُصلِّح	To drink	يشرب	To make	يصنع
To repeat	يكرر	To divide	يُقَسِّمُ	To work	يشتغل
To do	يعمل/يفعل	To publish	ينشر	To leave	يترك

(1) What is he doing at the present time?

- He is repeating his lesson in the classroom.

(2) What is she doing in the kitchen?

- She is cooking our food in the kitchen.

(3) What are they doing now?

- They are drinking orange juice.

(4) What are you doing?

- I am taking my lunch.

(5) What is he doing?

- He is publishing the news in the newspaper.

(6) What is she doing?

- She is leaving for London.

زمن الماضي المستمر

Past Continuous Tense

تُستعمل هذه الصيغة في الماضي للتعبير عن حدث أو عمل كان مستمراً في زمن الماضي عندما

وقع عمل أو حدث آخر واستمر بعده. وتتكون هذه الصيغة من فعل الكينونة في الماضي (was and

were) مع إضافة مقطع مكوّن من ثلاثة حروف (ing) إلى الفعل المراد استعماله مع الكلمات التالية:

Past Progressive Tense:

While	بينما / عندما / أثناء
Where	أين
When	مثل / بينما / أثناء
What?	ماذا / أداة سؤال (أو ما)
Who?	مَنْ / أداة سؤال للشخص ويستعمل (who) لربط الجملة.

وكما شرحنا في الدرس الخاص بصيغة المضارع المستمر يوضع: الضمير أولاً وفعل الكينونة ثانياً

وثالثاً الفعل المراد استعماله بإضافة (ing) في آخره.

Example: مثل:

(1) While he was swimming (يعوم) in the pool, his father came to see him.

أو في الجملة التالية:

(2) As he was swimming in the pool, his father came to see him.

المعنى واحد في كلا الجملتين.

بينما كان يعوم في الحوض، جاء أبوه ليراه.

(3) He was getting his usual food when his father came to tell him good news.

كان يتناول طعامه المألوف، عندما جاء أبوه ليخبره عن أخبار طيبة (usual) تنطق (iujual) وهي صفة تأتي قبل الإسم.

What was Ali doing when you saw him?

He was drinking his cup of tea when I saw him.

He was driving his new car when I saw him.

He was making (a lot of) noise in the class.

He was writing his new book on France.

He was working in the restaurant when I saw him.

Last night my father came in my room while I was reading a new letter.

The teacher came in the classroom, while the pupils were playing football.

We finished our lesson as the headmaster was coming with his guest in the classroom.

I saw my brother with his wife while I was driving my car to the station yesterday.

Where were you staying last night?

I was staying in the hotel (for my dinner).

Where was Ali staying? He was staying in the house.

New Words			كلمات جديدة
1- letter	حرف/ رسالة	5- guest	ضيف
2- pupils	تلاميذ	6- wife	زوجة
3- headmaster	مدير مدرسة	7- station	محطة
4- with	مع / حرف جر	8- a lot of	وافر/ كميّة من

Exercise (13):

(a) Change the Verbs into the

Present Continuous Tense:

تمرين (13):

غَيِّر الأفعال التالية

إلى صيغة الاستمرار في الحاضر

1- She (sits) beside the fire all day.

2- We (learn) our lessons very well.

3- You (speak) English very slow.

4- I (go) to sleep early today.

5- They (play) fooball in the garden.

6- Ali (takes) his bicycle for a trip.

7- Layla (tells) her story to her friend.

8- They (drink) milk before they (go) to school.

(b) Change the Verbs into the

Past Continuous Tense:

غَيِّر الأفعال التالية

إلى صيغة الاستمرار في الماضي:

1- She (sat) beside the fire (all day) (النهار كله).

2- We (learned) our lessons very well.

3- You (spoke) English very slow.

4- I (went) to sleep early today.

5- They (played) football in the garden.

6- Ali (took) his bicycle for a trip.

7- Yousef and Salwa (read) their book (red).

8- They (drank) milk before they went to school.

(a) New words:

كلمات جديدة:

Greetings	ترحيب/سلام/ تحية
Greet	يُرحب/يحي – فعل
Peace upon you	السلام عليكم
In the name of Most Gracious, Most Merciful God.	بسم الله الرحمن الرحيم
Goodbye	وداعاً/ أستودعكم الله
If you please	من فضلك/لو سمحت/أرجوك
Help yourself	تفضل/أخدم نفسك
By God!	و الله/بالله/للتعجب
God willing	إن شاء الله

Field	حقل – اسم
Airplane	طائرة
Mistake	خطأ/ غلط – اسم
Bell	جرس
Homework	واجب منزلي
Idea	فكرة/ رأي
Store	مخزن
Shop	حانوت
Will you please	لو سمحت/ من فضلك/أرجوك
God forbid!	لا قدر الله/ لا سمح الله
Awful	مرعب/مروّع
Is there any news today?	هل هناك/أو هل من جديد؟

Sentences with new verbs:

جمل بأفعال جديدة:

1- He will become wise at the end of his studies.

2- He became wiser as he grew older.

3- He has become a good pupil in class.

4- She begins very early to cook her food.

5- She began to go to school last year.

6- We have begun to make our new field.

7- They will begin work soon tomorrow.

8- His mother began to worry when her boy did not come last night.

9- We all began reading our lesson yesterday.

10- The nervous boy bites his fingernail.

11- my dog never bites.

New words	الكلمات الجديدة	New words	الكلمات الجديدة
at the end of	عند نهاية	soon	عاجلاً
his studies	دروسه	to worry	يشغل البال
wise	عاقل/ حكيم	did not come	لم يأتي
wiser	أكثر حكمة	all	كلنا /جميعاً
grew – grow	نمى / ينمو	nervous	عصبي
has become	قد أصبح/ صار	finger	اصبع
old – older	كبير / أكبر / صفة	fingers	أصابع
she begins	تبدأ / تشرع	fingernail	ظفر
early	مبكراً/ باكراً	fingernails	أظافر / جمع
never	أبداً/مطلقاً	nevermore	بعد اليوم أبداً

زمن المستقبلLesson Sixteen

Future Tense

لا بـد مـن مراجعـة فعـل الكينونـة (Verb to be) وفعـل الملكيـة (Verb to have) في حـالتي المستقبل والمضارع البسيط مع جميع تمريناتها المختلفة بحيث يمكن بعد ذلك المضي بـسهولة في شرح مـا هو المقصود من فعل المستقبل المستمر. ونجـد أن هـذا الفعـل (Future Continuous) والمقصود مـن استعماله هو استمرارية الفعل أو الحدث في زمن المستقبل غير القريب. ويتكـون (Future continuous) من الفعلين المساعدين وهما (Verb to be + will/shall) المصدر + الفعل المراد استعماله منتهياً بـ (ing) مثل:

Example:

1- (a) I shall go to the station. (Future simple tense)

(b) I shall be going to the station. (Future continuous)

2- (a) I am writing this lesson now.

(b) I shall be writing this lesson afterwards.

3- (a) He is studying English now.

(b) He will be studying German afterwards.

4- (a) We will have a new car today.

(b) We will be having a new car next week.

5- (a) Amira has an old car.

(b) Amira will be having a new car tomorrow.

الأفعالLesson Seventeen

القياسية والأفعال الشاذة

Regular & Irregular Verbs

الأفعال القياسية: 1- Regular Verbs:

نعود في هذا الدرس لإدراج بعض من الأفعال القياسية (Regular Verbs) التي تخضع لقوانين

لصياغتها في الماضي وذلك بإضافة حرف (d) أو (ed) أو (t) أو بتغيير مصدر الفعل المنتهي بحرف (y)

وقبله حرف ساكن إلى (ied) مثل: يدرس (study) درس إلى (studied) ويقلق (worry) قلق أو انزعج إلى

(worried) مع الانتباه إلى نطق الأفعال في الماضي جيداً.

لاحظ أن الأفعال التي تنتهي بالحروف (p – k – f – s – ch – sh) ويكون نطقها جميعاً في

زمن الماضي وكأنها حرف (t) مثل الأفعال التالية:

hope	يأمل	hoped	أمل	hoped	النطق	ث
like	يرغب	liked	رغب	liket	النطق	ث
laugh	يضحك	laughed	ضحك	laughet	النطق	ث
kiss	يقبّل	kissed	قبّل	kisset	النطق	ث
pitch	يطلي	pitched	طلى	pitchet	النطق	ث
fish	يصطاد	fished	اصطاد	fished	النطق	ث

والأفعال المنتهية بحرف (ed) أو (t) مثل الأفعال التالية يكون نطقها (id) (إذْ) مثل:

visit	يزور	visited	زار	visitid	النطق	إذْ
want	يريد	wanted	أراد	wantid	النطق	إذْ
need	يحتاج	needed	احتاج	nidid	النطق	إذْ

Regular Verbs

الأفعال القياسية

1 Present Tense	2 Past Tense	3 Past Participle	المعنى
ask	asked	asked	يسأل
assist	assisted	assisted	يساعد / يعاون
assure	assured	assured	يتأكد
accept	accepted	accepted	يقبل
aid	aided	aided	يسعف
acquire	acquired	acquired	يحرز / ينال
arrest	arrested	arrested	يقبض على
answer	answered	answered	يجاوب / يرد
address	addressed	addressed	يُعَنْون
amuse	amused	amused	يُسَلِّي / يلهي
exact	exacted	exacted	يصحح/يدقق/يبتز
aim	aimed	aimed	يهدف
arranged	arranged	arranged	يُرتِّب
allow	allowed	allowed	يسمح

84

advertise	advertised	advertised	يعلن
appear	appear	appeared	يظهر للعيان
blame	blamed	blamed	يلوم
brush	brushed	brushed	ينظف / يفرك
burn	burned	burned	يحرق
blush	blush	blushed	يحمر وجهه
believe	believed	believed	يصدق / يعتقد
behave	behaved	behaved	يسلك / يتصرف
borrow	borrowed	borrowed	يَسْتَلف / يقترض
board	boarded	boarded	يركب متن السفينة
bleach	bleached	bleached	يبيض
balance	balance	balanced	يوازن
boil	boiled	boiled	يغلي الماء
bother	bothered	bothered	يربك
content	contented	contented	مُطْمَئِن / يقنع
console	consoled	consoled	يعزي / يواسي
close	closed	closed	يقفل
consider	considered	considered	يفكر في / يدرس
carry	carried	carried	يحمل / ينقل
complete	completed	completed	يتمم / تام / منجز
cross	crossed	crossed	يشطب/يقطع الطريق

call	called	called	يصيح/يصرخ/ينادي
contain	contained	contained	يحتوي/يتضمن
count	counted	counted	يعد / يحصي
care	cared	cared	يهتم / يحرص
control	controlled	controlled	يفحص / يستنبط
continue	continued	continued	يستمر / يدوم/يمتد
cook	cooked	cooked	يطبخ / يطهو
convey	conveyed	conveyed	ينقل / يوصل
cover	covered	covered	يحمي / يخفي /' يستر
climb	climbed	climbed	يتسلق
defend	defended	defended	يحمي/يصون/يدافع
desert	deserted	deserted	يهجر / يترك
delay	delayed	delayed	يؤجل/يؤخر/يعيق
demand	demanded	demanded	يطلب/يطالب بـ
depart	departed	departed	يسافر/يرحل/يموت
dry	dried	dried	يجف / يجفف
delight	delighted	delighted	يبتهج
dream	dreamed	dreamed	يحلم
desire	desired	desired	يرغب في / يتوق إلى
divide	divided	divided	يقسم
discover	discovered	discovered	يكتشف

decide	decided	decided	يقرر
dance	danced	danced	يرقص
dictate	dictated	dictated	يملي/يأمر
describe	described	described	يصف/يصور/يرسم
differ	differed	differed	يختلف معه
declare	declared	declared	يعلن / يصرح بـ
die	died	died	يموت / يخمد
extend	extended	extended	يبسط / ينشر
explain	explained	explained	يفسر / يشرح
examine	examined	examined	يمتحن / يختبر
enter	entered	entered	يدخل
enjoy	enjoyed	enjoyed	يتمتع / يتنعم بـ
expect	expected	expected	يتوقع
excite	excited	excited	يثير / يستفز
end	ended	ended	ينهي
express	expressed	expressed	يعبر عن
encourage	encouraged	encouraged	يشجع / يستحث
include	included	included	يشتمل / يتضمن
exchange	exchanged	exchanged	يُبادل/ يقايض
escape	escaped	escaped	يفلت من / ينجو
extinguish	extinguished	extinguished	يطفئ/ يخمد

finish	finished	finished	ينهي/يكمل
fulfill	fulfilled	fulfilled	ينفذ/ينجز
fill	filled	filled	يملأ/يصب
fire	fired	fired	يشعل/ينير
follow	followed	followed	يتبع/يلاحق
guess	guessed	guessed	يخمّن/يحزر
growl	growled	growled	يهدر/يتذمر
gleam	gleamed	gleamed	يومض
grant	granted	granted	يمنح/يوافق
grumble	grumbled	grumbled	يتذمر/يدمدم
gain	gained	gained	يكسب/يربح
guarantee	guaranteed	guaranteed	يضمن/يكفل
grudge	grudged	grudged	يشكو/يتذمر
gather	gathered	gathered	يجمع/يحشد
gaze	gazed	gazed	يحدق/يتفرس
help	help	helped	يساعد/يعاون
happen	happened	happened	يقع/يحدث
hope	hoped	hoped	يأمل
hurry	hurried	hurried	يسرع
handle	handled	handled	يلمس/يمسك
inherit	inherited	inherited	يورث

insist	insisted	insisted	يصر/يلح
inform	informed	informed	يبلغ/يخبر
injure	injured	injured	يظلم/يجرح
imagine	imagined	imagined	يتصور/يتخيل
inspect	inspected	inspected	يفحص/يعاين
introduce	introduced	introduced	يقدم/يضع مقدمة
kill	killed	killed	يقتل
kiss	kissed	kissed	يقبّل
kedge	kedged	kedged	يجر السفينة
key	keyed	keyed	يغلق بمفتاح
kick	kicked	kicked	يرفس/يقاوم/يضرب
kindle	kindled	kindled	يضرم النار
knife	knifed	knifed	يطعن/يقطع
laugh	laughed	laughed	يضحك
like	liked	liked	يحب/يرغب
look for	looked for	looked for	يبحث عن
live	lived	lived	يعيش
learn	learned	learned	يتعلم
land	landed	landed	يهبط / ينزل
listen	listened	listened	يستمع/يصغي
lay	laid	laid	يضع

lie	lied	lied	يكذب
load	loaded	loaded	يشحن/يُحَمِّل
lie	lay	lain	يرقد/يتمدد
love	loved	loved	يحب/يعشق
miss	missed	missed	يفتقد/يتجنب
move	moved	moved	يتحرك
mark	marked	marked	يؤشر/يُعَيِّن
mail	mailed	mailed	يرسل بالبريد
need	needed	needed	يحتاج
notice	noticed	noticed	يلاحظ/يشير إلى
offer	offered	offered	يقدم/يُبدي
open	opened	opened	يفتح
own	owned	owned	يملك/يقر
occur	occurred	occurred	يحدث/يوجد
observe	observed	observed	يلاحظ/يتقيد
obtain	obtained	obtained	يحرز/يحصل على
pressure	pressured	pressured	يضغط على
please	pleased	pleased	يفرِّح
participate	participated	participated	يشارك
petrify	petrified	petrified	يُحَجِّر/يُحَوِّل إلى حجر
punish	punished	punished	يعاقب

90

pardon	pardoned	pardoned	يسامح
promise	promised	promised	يُوعد/يتعهد بـ
play	played	played	يعلب/يعزف
plant	planted	planted	يزرع/يغرس
pour	poured	poured	يسكب/يصب
pull	pulled	pulled	يجذب
permit	permitted	permitted	يأذن
provide	provided	provided	يزود/يوفر
present	presented	presented	يقدم/يعرض
place	placed	placed	يضع
print	printed	printed	يطبع
pitch	pitched	pitched	يقذف
persuade	persuaded	persuaded	يقنع
protect	protected	protected	يحمي
publish	published	published	ينشر
question	questioned	questioned	يستفسر
quarrel	quarreled	quarreled	يتعارك
qualify	qualified	qualified	يُؤهِل/يفوِّض
quench	quenched	quenched	يطفئ/يتغلب
quicken	quickened	quickened	يُنَشِّط/يُعَجِّل
quiet	quieted	quieted	يهدأ/يُهْدِئ

repay	repaid	repaid	يجازي/يكافئ
reach	reached	reached	يصل
request	requested	requested	يطلب
rain	rained	rained	تمطر
return	returned	returned	يرجع/يعود
realize	realized	realized	يتحقق
result	resulted	resulted	ينتج
require	required	required	يتطلب
remember	remembered	remembered	يتذكر
rule	ruled	ruled	يحكم
raise	raised	raised	يرفع/يُعلي
rent	rented	rented	يؤجِّر
recognize	recognized	recognized	يتعرف على
remain	remained	remained	يبقى
retain	retained	retained	يحافظ
repair	repaired	repaired	يُصلح
received	received	received	يَسْتلم
rest	rested	rested	يستريح/يهدأ
support	supported	supported	يدعم
smile	smile	smiled	يبتسم
stretch	stretched	stretched	يمدد

study	studied	studied	يدرس
stop	stopped	stopped	يتوقف
sound	sounded	sounded	يردد/يُرجِّع
suppose	supposed	supposed	يفترض
sail	sailed	sailed	يُبحر
save	saved	saved	يدخر
seem	seemed	seemed	يبدو
show	showed	showed	يعرض/يُبيِّن
shout	shouted	shouted	يصيح
shave	shaved	shaved	يحلق الذقن
suffocate	suffocated	suffocated	يختنق
start	started	started	يبدأ
serve	served	served	يخدم/يَقدم شيء
surround	surrounded	surrounded	يحيط
suffer	suffered	suffered	يعاني
translate	translated	translated	يترجم
thank	thanked	thanked	يشكر
try	tried	tried	يجرِّب
travel	traveled	traveled	يسافر
talk	talked	talked	يتحدث
trouble	troubled	troubled	يزعج/يقلق

trust	trusted	trusted	يثق/يأمل
turn	turned	turned	يحرك/يلوي
type	typed	typed	يطبع/يُرمِّز
use	used	used	يستعمل
unfasten	unfastened	unfastened	يفك/يحل
unfetter	unfettered	unfettered	يحرر (من الأغلال)
unfold	unfolded	unfolded	ينشر/يكشف
unite	united	united	يوحد/يربط
visit	visited	visited	يزور/يتفقد
view	viewed	viewed	يشاهد/يفحص
violate	violated	violated	ينتهك (حرمة)
voice	voiced	voiced	يعبّر عن/ يلفظ
wonder	wondered	wondered	يتعجَّب
want	wanted	wanted	يريد/يرغب
welcome	welcomed	welcomed	يرحب
work	worked	worked	يخدم/يعمل
waste	wasted	wasted	يضيع/يُبَدِّد
walk	walked	walked	يمشي/يسير
wash	washed	washed	يغسل/يزيل
watch	watched	watched	يراقب/يشاهد

2- Irregular Verbs: الأفعال الشاذة:

1 Present Tense	2 Past Tense	3 Past Participle	المعنى
dig	dug	dug	يحفر/يستخرج
do – does	did	done	يفعل/يعمل
draw	drew	drawn	يجر/يسحب
dream	dreamt (ed)	dreamt (ed)	يحلم
drink	drank	drunk	يشرب
drive	drove	driven	يقود
dwell	dwelt	dwelt	يسكن/يقطن
eat	ate	eaten	يأكل
fall	fell	fallen	يسقط
feed	fed	fed	يغذي/يطعم
feel	felt	felt	يشعر/يحس
fight	fought	fought	يتقاتل/يتشاجر
find	found	found	يجد/يلقى
flee	fled	fled	يفر/يتفادى
fly	flew	flown	يطير
forbid	forbade	forbidden	يحظر/يحرّم/يمنع
forget	forgot	forgotten	ينسى
forgive	forgave	forgiven	يغفر/يصفح

95

Exercise (14):

تمرين (14):

(a) Put the following sentences

ضع الجمل الآتية في زمن

into present continuous Tense:

زمن المضارع المستمر:

1- I dig a hole. ....

2- We do our homework. ....

3- You draw your cheques. ....

4- She drinks water. ....

5- It drives out its kittens. ....

6- You dwell in town. ....

7- He dreams at night. ....

8- They eat only meat. ....

(b) Put the following sentences

ضع الجمل الآتية في حالة

into negative:

نفي:

1- I dug a hole. ....

2- We did our homework. ....

3- You drew your cheques. ....

4- She drank water. ....

5- It drove out its kittens. ....

6- You dwelt in town. ....

7- He dreamt at night. ....

8 They ate only meat. ....

الدرس الثامن عشر

حروف الجر

Propositions

لاحظ: أن حروف الجر (The Prepositions) تشكل في اللغة الإنجليزية بعض الـصعوبات ولا

سيما لمن لم يدرس استعمالاتها المختلفة دراسة جيدة لفهـم معانيها في الجملـة. هنـا وتُبين حـروف الجر

حسب موضع استعمالها العلاقة بينها وبين (1) الإسم و(2) الفعل و(3) الصفة. مثال في هذه الجمل الثلاثة:

(1) I have a (house of) six rooms.

عندي بيت من (6) حجرات.

(2) He (went in) the room.

دخل في الحجرة.

(3) Ali has (a good car)

علي عنده سيارة جيدة،

(at) the station.

عند أو في المحطة.

Example:

لاحظ أن لكل حرف جر استعمالاته الخاصة مثل:

(at)

عند/في/إلى/نحو/في حالة/ بسعر/ على

The car is (at) home.

السيارة عند البيت أو في البيت

He comes (at) noon.

يأتي عند الظهر

I study English (at) the university.

أدرس الإنجليزية في الجامعة

Wait (at) the school today.

انتظر عند المدرسة اليوم

Ali sleeps (at) 9 o'clock.

علي يرقد عند الساعة التاسعة

We bought this book (at) 5 dinars.

اشترينا هذا الكتاب بسعر بخمس دينارات.

I play (in) the field.

العب في الحقل

He wants (to) go home now.

يريد أن يذهب إلى منزله الآن

Layla comes (to) the school early (in) the morning).

ليلى تأتي إلى المدرسة مبكراً في الصباح

He came (by) train.

جاء بواسطة القطار (عن طريق)

New words	كلمات جديدة	New words	كلمات جديدة
the crowd	حشد/مجموعة	vacancy	فراغ أو عطلة
the world	العالم/الدنيا	variety	تنوع
the sun	الشمس	vulgarity	مسلك سوقي
cheerful	مرح/مبتهج	target	هدف
rain	مطر	avail	يفيد/فائدة/نافع
winter	الشتاء	pardon	معذرة/عفو
summer	الصيف	storage	مخزن/مستودع
spring	الربيع	gold	ذهب
autumn	الخريف	silver	فضة
collar	طوق	verbally	حرفياً
tall	عالٍ، طويل	orally	شفهياً (لفظ فمي)
building	العمارة	job	شغل/واجب/عمل

club	نادٍ	item	مادة في القانون/شيء
member	عضو	claim	مطالبة بشيء
first	الأول	football team	فريق كرة قدم
second	الثاني	reward	مكافأة
third	الثالث	burden	حمل
stranger	غريب	the moon	القمر
foreigner	أجنبي	the sky	السماء
seasons	الفصول	blackboard	اللوح/سبورة
journey	رحلة	chalk	طباشير
near	قريب	beside	بجانب

Prepositions:

about	عن/حول	around	حول/حوالي	down	تحت
above	فوق/آنفاً	at	عند/في حالة	for	لأجل
after	بعد/في أثر	before	قبل/من قبل	from	من
against	ضد/نحو	behind	وراء/في المؤخرة	in	في
along	على طول	beside	بجانب/بقرب	into	في/نحو/داخل
among	ما بين	by	بواسطة	near	قريب
of	أداة إضافة	out of	خرج	through	من خلال

off	بعيد عن	over	فوق	to	إلى
on	على	round	حول/طوال	under	تحت
upon	فوق/على	with	مع	without	من غير/بدون

ملاحظة: هامة بشأن حروف الجر ومعانيها عند استعمالها. ولقد أدرجتُ بعضاً منها والتي تعتبر أكثر الحروف المتداولة، غير أن معانيها المختلفة باللغة العربية ليست في الحقيقة كافية في هذه الأعمدة وعليه يجب على الدّارس أن يطلع على أي قاموس جيد للبحث عن المزيد من المعاني وكيفية استعمالها. ولنأخذ مثلاً حرف الجر (at - عند).

at	عند/إلى/في	at least	على الأقل
at noon	عند الظهر	come at once	تعال حالاً
at home	في البيت	she came	جاءت
aim at	صوب إلى	at once	في الحال
the target	الهدف	at the most	على الأكثر
at war	في حالة حرب	let it go	اتركه على حاله أو
he came	جاء	at that	تقبل ذلك الأمر
at last	أخيراً		من غير مناقشة

Prepositions:

What are you at?	ماذا تفعل/ما الذي تفعله؟
Steel is made from iron.	الفولاذ مصنوع من الحديد.
I want money from him.	أُريد نقوداً منه.
Count three days from today is holiday.	عد ثلاثة أيام من اليوم يكون عطلة/استراحة.
I am suffering from cold.	أتألّم من البرد.
Come with me in the class.	تعال معي في الفصل.
Behind the scenes.	وراء الكواليس/ الستار.
He was with his friend.	كان مع صديقه.
Castles in the air.	قصور في الهواء.
Do as we do (as = مثل/كما).	اعمل كما نعمل نحن.
Stories of my travels.	قصص عن رحلاتي.
Castles of sand.	قصور من الرمال.
The book is under the table.	الكتاب تحت الطاولة.
He was talking about the lesson.	كان يتكلم عن الدرس.
I want to wait here till/until he comes from the school.	أريد أن أنتظر هنا حتى/ إلى غاية/ يأتي من المدرسة.
He went in/into the house.	دخل البيت/المنزل.
You are behind time.	أنت تأخرت/أنت متأخر.
He is behind in his payments.	متأخر في تسديد مدفوعاته.
This money is between me and you.	هذه النقود هي بيني وبينك.

101

Prepositions:

A house of six rooms.	منزل من ست حجرات.
He drove the man off my house.	ساق الرجل بعيداً من منزلي.
He came home off and on.	أتى إلى المنزل بين فترة وأُخرى.
She is well off.	هي غنيّة.
He is badly off.	هو في حالة عُسر مالي.
Be off.	إذهب بعيداً.
Put off your question today.	أخِّر/أجِّل سؤَالك اليوم.
The fish you saw is a bit off.	السمك الذي رأيته غير طازج.
This news is off the record.	هذه الأخبار ليست للنشر.
The man was upstairs.	كان الرجل في الدور العلوي (فوق).
My room is upstairs.	حجرتي في الدور العلوي (فوق).
His room is downstairs.	حجرته في الدور السفلي (تحت).
He traveled by car yesterday.	سافر بواسطة السيارة أمس.
It is high time for us to go home now.	آن لنا أن نذهب إلى المنزل الآن.
He read the book from early morning until/till late at night.	قرأ الكتاب من الصباح باكراً حتى/إلى غاية الليل متأخراً.
He waited until the man came home.	انتظر حتى/إلى غاية أن جاء الرجل إلى المنزل.
We always go to Jordan by train or by bus.	دائماً نذهب إلى الأردن بواسطة القطار أو بواسطة الحافلة.

Exercise (15):

Put the suitable preposition

In the blank space.

(1) We catch fish ……….. the river.

(2) He goes ……… a holiday ………. his farm.

(3) I always lie ……… my bed ……….. read a book.

(4) They live ……. Beirut ……… sometime.

(5) I was born ……… Beirut but I live …….. Saida.

(6) There is no mistake ……… my exercise ………. today.

(7) I got ……….. six o'clock this morning.

(8) Ali saw this picture ………… the cinema last night.

(9) He went ………. school …………. his brother today.

(10) They sat …….. these chairs ………. the fire.

(11) The student came ………. school very early today.

(12) They learn English ……… the school.

(13) Tell me ……… your story. The sky is …….. our heads.

(14) He drove the dog ………. . The book is ……. the table.

(15) Your bag is ……. the table. Come …….. me today.

(16) Ali played …….. his brother. There is a house ……. the river.

(17) I wrote my homework ……. Friday. He came …….. you.

(18) My room is …………. His room is ……….

(19) Amira goes ………. the market …….. her car.

(20) Layla is talking …… the class …….. her exercises.

Lesson Nineteen　　　　　　　　　　　　　الدرس التاسع عشر

الأفعال المساعدة

The Auxiliary Verbs

الأفعال المساعدة هي أفعال لا تحتاج إلى فعل آخر لأجل تكوين السؤال أو النفي لأنها من نفس هـذه الأفعال يتكون منها السؤال أو النفي وذلك بوضع أداة النفي (not) بعـد الفعـل مبـاشرة أو يوضـع الفعـل قبل الضمير أو الاسم في حالة السؤال:

The Auxiliary Verbs - المضارع	الماضي	الترجمة
1- Verb to be: am – is – are	was - were	كان / كانوا
2- Verb to have: have – has	had	كان عنده
3- Verb: shall - سوف	should	تستعمل للواجب وللأمر
4- Verb: will - سوف	would	يريد/يرغب/يتمنى
5- Verb: can – يقدر/يستطيع	could	يستطيع
6- Verb: may – يقدر/يمكنه	might	يستطيع/يتمكن
7- Verb: must	-	يفيد معنى للواجب
8- Verb: have to – يجب/لازم	had to	كان يجب أن
9- Verb: has to – يجب/لازم	had to	كان يجب أن
10- Verb: will be able to	would be able to	سوف يكون قادراً
11- Verb: shall be able to	should be able to	سوف يكون قادراً
12- Verb: ought to – ينبغي على	-	يجب/يُسْتَحْسن/يلزم
13- Verb: do – does يفعل	did	يفعل/يعمل

Auxiliary Verbs:

أفعال مساعدة:

فعل (should) يلفظ (shood) وفعل (would) يلفظ (would). وينطبق على جميع الأفعال المساعدة عملية الاختصار في المحادثة فقط.

Example:

مثل:

Affirmative	Negative	المختصر المضارع	المختصر الماضي
can	can not	can't	couldn't
shall	shall not	shan't	shouldn't
will	will not	won't	wouldn't
may	may not	mayn't	mightn't
must	must not	mustn't	لا يوجد ماضي
ought to	ought not to	mustn't	لا يوجد ماضي
have to	have not to	haven't to	hadn't to
has to	has not to	hasn't to	hadn't to
shall be able to	shall not be able to	shan't be able to	shouldn't be able to
will be able to	will not be able to	won't be able to	wouldn't be able to

You can read English.	You cannot read English.
You could write English.	You could not write English.
I may ride a bicycle.	I may not ride a bicycle.
I might ride a bicycle.	I might not ride a bicycle.
The waiter must come here.	The waiter must not come here.
I shall like to go there.	I shall not like to go there.
I should like to go there.	I should not like to go there.
I should like to see somebody.	I should not like to see anybody.

Auxiliary Verbs:

هناك استعمالات خاصة للأفعال المساعدة (Auxiliary Verbs) منها:

(1) يُستعمل فعل (should) ويلفظ (shood) للتعبير عن الواجب مثل: قلتُ أنه يجب أن آتي في الأسبوع المقبل.

I said that I should come next week.

(2) وللتعبير عن الشك أو شيء ما مشكوك فيه مثل: إذا أمطرت، يجب ألا أذهب أو يجب ألا أذهب لـو أمطرت.

If it rains, I should not go.

I should not go, if it rains.

(3) للتعبير عن شيء كاد أن يحدث ولكنه لم يحدث مثل: كنت أن أذهب سألتني / كنت أن أكون ذاهباً لو سألتني.

I should have gone, if you asked me.

استعمالات فعل (Would):

(1) يستعمل فعل (would) ويلفظ (wood) للرغبة أي مثلاً يكون راغباً/ لو أنهم رغبوا في ذلك He would if they would (يكون راغباً في الذهاب لو أنهم رغبوا في ذلك).

(2) وللتعبير عن الإرادة أو التصميم: He would go in spite of your warning (قد صمم على الذهاب رغـماً عن إنذارك).

(3) للتعبير عن تكرار شيء ما مثل عمل/لعب/ قراءة إلخ.

The children would play for hours in their field.

يرغب الأطفال اللعب لساعات في حقلهم.

(4) وللتعبير عن الأماني مثل:

أتمنى أن أكون غنياً! I would, I were rich – I would (if) I were rich!

ليته كان هنا! Would that he were here!

(5) وللتعبير عن أي طلب مساعدة مثل:

Would you help me, please? (Please help me!)

لو سَمَحْت تساعدني من فضلك؟

استعمالات فعل (must):

(1) فعل (must) يستعمل للتعبير عن الواجب أو شيء ضروري مثل:

All men must eat to live. الإنسان يجب أن يأكل ليعيش.

You must keep your promise. يجب أن تحافظ على وعدك.

You must read your lesson every day. يجب أن تقرأ درسك يومياً.

(2) للتعبير عن شيء يجب ألا يُهمل.

The man must be crazy to do so. الرجل لا بد أن يكون مجنوناً أن يقوم بمثل هـذا الشيء.

This boy must be crazy to read this story. هذا الولد لا بد أنه مخبول أن يقرأ هـذه الرواية/ القصة.

(1) فعل (ought to) يلفظ (oot) يُستعمل للواجب أو للضرورة مثل: must.

You ought to obey your parents.

يجب عليك أن تحترم والديك.

Vagabondage ought not to be allowed.

لا يمكن/يجب ألّا يُترك أو يُسمح للتشرد/التشرد.

(2) للتعبير عن التعقل أو الحكمة/ تأمل أو تروي (في الأمر) مثل:

I ought to go before it rains.

يجب/يُستحسن أن أذهب قبل أن تُمطر.

I must go before it rains.

لا بد أن أذهب قبل أن تُمطر.

(3) للتعبير عن التوقع من حدوث شيء ما مثل:

At your age you ought to know this bad story.

في سنك/ في هذا العمر يجب أن تعرف هذه القصة الرديئة.

It ought to be a fine day tomorrow.

لا بد أن يكون غداً جميلاً.

(1) فعل (may) يستعمل للتعبير عن السماح أو عن الإمكانية بأي شيء مثل:

May I have an apple?

هل في الإمكان الحصول على تفاحة؟

May I have an orange juice?

هل في الإمكان الحصول على عصير برتقال؟

May I have a glass of water?

هل في الإمكان الحصول على كباية ماء؟

May I go now?

هل يمكن أن أذهب؟

It may rain tomorrow.

يمكن/ربما تمطر غداً.

It may rain tomorrow.

من المحتمل أن تمطر غداً.

The train may be late.

يمكن أن يتأخر القطار/يحتمل تأخير القطار.

(2) للتعبير عن الأمل أو الرجاء مثل:

أرجو/أتمنى لك يوماً جميلاً.   May you have a nice day.

أتمنى لك رحلة طيبة/أرجو لك.   May you have a good trip.

(1) فعل (might) يلفظ (mait) وهو ماضٍ لفعل (may) يُستعمل للتعبير عـن الإذن/ السماح في صيغة الكلام المباشر وسوف نتحدث عنها في الدروس المقبلة.

Father said: «You may play in the farm today».

Father said that I might play in the farm today.

1- كلمة (that) تعني (أن).

الوالد قال إنك في الإمكان أن تلعب في الحقل اليوم.

(2) وللتعبير عن الاحتمال بعمل أي شيء كما في هذا التعبير: كـان مـن المحتمـل أن يفعلـه عنـدما لم تكـن تراه.

He might have done it when you were not looking.

Exercise (16):   تمـرين (16): Put the sentences into (a) question

(b) into negative.

ضع هذه الجمل أولاً في حالة سؤال وثانياً في حالة نفي.

1- I can read English well.

2- I am able to read English well.

3- I could read English well.

4- I was able to read English well.

5- I shall be able to read English well next week.

6- I should be able to read English well if I did all the exercises.

7- He will be able to read English well if he did all the exercises.

8- He would be able to read English well if he did all the exercises.

9- The tree will bear fruit next month.

10- He will tell me about the story tomorrow.

11- He would tell me about it next day.

12- I have found your book in my desk.

13- I shall hear you. This reading is right.

14- They must answer all the exercises well.

15- I shall answer this question after the lesson.

16- You will find the pupils in the class.

17- This story will be forgotten.

18- You will be able to tell me the whole story.

19- He could tell you the story.

20- The train ought to be here now.

21- You must be patient.

22- They will be all soldiers next month.

Lesson Twenty

الدرس العشرون

زمن المضارع التام

The Present Perfect Tense

(1) يستعمل زمن المضارع التام لعمل أو لحدث قد تم أو أُنجز في وقت ما دون تحديد الـزمن الـذي وقـع

فيه لأن الاهتمام واقع في حالة الحدث الراهن.

(2) تستعمل مع هذه الصيغة الكلمات التالية:

1- since	(منذ ذلك الوقت) (ever since) و(منذ)
2- already	الآن/قبل الآن/في ذلك الحين/ قبل هذا الوقت
3- just	منذ لحظات/ منذ لحظة
4- only	فقط/وحيد
5- for	منذ/المدة/لأجل/الآن
6- yet	حتى الآن/لأن
7- not yet	لا زال (للنفي)
8- lately	حديثاً/ منذ عهد قريب
9- recently	مؤخراً/حديثاً
10- this week	هذا الأسبوع
11- this month	هذا الشهر
12- this year	هذا العام

(3) ويتكون زمن المضارع التام (Present Perfect Tense) مـن فعـل (have) للجمـع مـع اسـم الفاعـل
(past participle). وكذلك من فعل (has) للضمير المفرد مثل:

I have written two letters only.

كتبت رسالتين فقط قبل الآن

في هذه الجملة (في زمن المضارع التام) (Present Perfect Tense)، قد بيّنت العمل دون أن تحدد وقـت
إنهائه. وعليه لاحظ هذه الأمثلة:

The sun has been up since six.

أشرقت الشمس منذ السادسة

أي بدأ طلوع الشمس في الماضي وما زال حتى الآن مستمراً.

They have worked hard since they left school.

قد اشتغلوا بجد منذ أن تركوا المدرسة.

زمن الماضي التام Lesson Twenty One الدرس الحادي والعشرون

The Past Perfect Tense

يتكون هذا الفعل مــن (had) ســواء أكانـت الأسـماء في حالـة جمـع أو مفرد مـع اسـتعمال (before) أو

(after) مع اسم الفاعل (Past participle).

Example:

(a) I wrote my letters yesterday.

كتبتُ رسائلي أمس

في هذه الجملة حُدد وقت عملك بيوم أمس.

(b) I had written my letters (before) Ali came in my house.

لقد كتبت رسائلي قبل مجيء علي إلى منزلي. (لم تحدد وقت عملك).

(c) Ali came in my house (after) I had written my letters.

جاء علي إلى منزلي بعد أن كتبت رسائلي (بمعنى أن الرسائل كتبت قبل مجيء علي).

(1) القاعدة كـما في الجملتين: إذا أتى فعـلان في الـزمن الماضي، نضع زمـن الماضي التـام (Past Perfect

Tense) أولاً ثم نضع الماضي البسيط.

(2) تستعمل كلمة (before) بعد زمن الماضي التـام كـما هـو في المثـال حـرف (b) بيـنما تـستعمل كلمـة

(after) بعد فعل الماضي البسيط كما في الجملة حرف (c).

لاحظ هذه الجمل في المضارع والماضي التام:

(1) I have seen the teacher lately.

(2) We have read many books in these days.

(3) She has been here before two hours in the stations.

(1) I had seen the teacher before the bell rang.

(2) We had read many books before Ali read them.

(3) She had been here for two hours in the station.

زمن المستقبل التام

The Future Perfect Tense

(1) يُستعمل زمن المستقبل التام (Future Perfect Tense) للتعبير عن فعل سوف يكتمل حدوثه في زمن معين في المستقبل.

(a) I shall have written my letter before noon.   سوف أكون قد كتبت رسالتي قبل الظهر

(before noon)

(b) He will have written his letter by one   سوف يكون قد كتب رسالته في خلال ساعة.
o'clock.

(c) They will ride their bicycles at the end of   سوف يركبون دراجاتهم في نهاية الدرس.
the lessons. (at the end of)

(2) وتتكون هذه الصيغة (Future Perfect Tense) أولاً من الفعل المساعد (shall وwill) وثانياً من الفعل المساعد (have) وثالثاً من اسم الفاعل (Past Participle) المراد استعماله.

(3) ولأجل عملية نفي الجملة من فعلين نضع أداة النفي بعد الفعل المساعد الرئيسي.

Example: مثال:

I shall or will have bought a new car by the end of this month.

سوف أكون قد اشتريت سيارة جديدة بنهاية هذا الشهر.

117

I will have bought a new car by the end of this month.	سوف أكون قد اشتريت سيارة جديدة بنهاية هـذا الشهر.
You will have finished this work by tomorrow.	سوف تكون قد أنهيت هذا العمل خلال يوم الغد.
He will have read the lesson before one o'clock.	سوف يكون قد قرأ الدرس قبل الساعة الواحدة.
She will have answered her exercise by an hour.	سوف تكون قد أجابت على تمرينها خـلال/أثنـاء الساعة.
You will have arrived at the house by noon.	سوف تكونوا قد وصلتم إلى المنزل خلال الظهر.
We will have left our school by the time you get home.	سوف نكون قد تركنا المدرسة خـلال الوقـت الـذي تصل فيه المنزل.
They will have got their money by the end of December.	سوف يكونوا قد حصلوا على نقودهم بنهاية شهر ديسمبر.

زمن المضارع التام المستمر

The Present perfect continuous Tense

إن زمن المضارع التام المستمر يُستعمل للدلالة على امتداد الحدث في زمن الماضي حتى الحاضر. ويتكون:

(1) من الفعل المساعد (have) للجمع و(has) للمفرد بعد الاسم أو الضمير مباشرة.

(2) زائد التصريف الثالث لفعل (To Be) (been). (I have been).

(3) زائد الفعل المراد استعماله في زمن المضارع البسيط.

(3) زائد المقطع (ing) بحيث يضاف إلى الفعل المضارع البسيط. مثال:

Example:

I have been writing my lesson as the teacher told me.

كنت أكتب درسي كما قال لي المدرس.

وكما تستعمل الكلمات التالية مع المضارع التام المستمر:

all the morning	طوال الصباح
for five minutes	لمدة خمس دقائق
for a long time	لمدة طويلة
for two years	لمدة سنتين
for twenty years	لمدة عشرين سنة
too long	مدة طويلة جداً
for two hours	لمدة ساعتين

Present Perfect Continuous Tense:

Example: أمثلة حول زمن المضارع التام المستمر:

The fireplace has been smoking well for two hours.

They have been swimming in the pool all the morning.

We have been getting our food as your friend ordered.

She has been coming to the market for ten years.

He has been looking for some bread too long.

I have been listening to the radio all the day.

Ali has been knowing his lesson well today.

Amira has been staying in France too long.

Yousef has been driving his car for twenty years.

You have been doing your work for two days.

He has been doing his work all day long.

All day long he has been waiting for his car to come.

The train has been running all the morning.

The teacher has been teaching English for three hours.

He has been lying there for three hours.

ملاحظة هامة: أن كل هذه الجمل التي صيغت حسب زمن المضارع التام المستمر تبين التأكيد أن الحـدث لم ينقطع عند لحظة الكلام ويختلف عن صيغة المضارع المستمر.

زمن الماضي التام المستمر

The Past Perfect Continuous Tense

إن قاعدة زمن الماضي التام المستمر لا تختلف عن قاعدة زمن المضارع التام إلا لكونه يُستعمل في الماضي فقط. ويستعمل لتوضيح كم من وقت استغرقه حدث ما قبل وقوع حدث آخر في الماضي.

Example: مثال:

1- The fire place had been burning well for two hours.

1- كان قد اشتعل موقد النار جيداً لمدة ساعتين.

2- They had been swimming in the pool all the morning.

2- كانوا قد سبحوا في الحوض طوال الصباح.

3- We had been getting food as your friend ordered.

3- كنا قد حصلنا على الطعام كما/مثلما أمره صديقك.

4- She had been coming to the market for ten years.

4- كانت قد أتت إلى السوق لمدة عشر سنوات.

ملاحظة: بالإمكان تكوين السؤال أو النفي سواء أكان للمضارع التام المستمر أو للماضي التام المستمر دون الحاجة إلى استعمال أي (أداة للسؤال) وذلك باتباع نفس القاعدة المتعلقة بالأفعال المساعدة التي أشرنا إليها سابقاً.

Example:	مثال:

(a) The fireplace had been burning for two hours.

كان قد اشتعل موقد النار جيداً لمدة ساعتين.

(b) Had the fire place been burning well for two hours?

هل كان قد اشتعل موقد النار جيداً لمدة ساعتين؟

The answer:

الجواب (بنعم أو لا):

Yes, it had been burning well for two hours.

أجل كان قد اشتعل موقد النار جيداً لمدة ساعتين.

No, it had not been burning well for two hours.

لا لم يكن قد اشتعل موقد النار جيدا لمدة ساعتين.

Question:

سؤال:

How had the fireplace been burning for two hours?

كيف (كان قد) اشتعل موقد النار لمدة ساعتين؟

The answer:

الجواب إما بالجملة الكاملة أو باختصارها:

It had been burning well or just (well) only.

كان قد اشتعل جيداً أو الاكتفاء بقولك (جيداً) فقط.

أنواع الصفات وعلاقاتها بالأسماء

Kinds of adjectives and nouns

تستعمل الصفة في اللغة الإنجليزية قبل الاسم مباشرة أو بعد فعل الكينونة (Verb to be) في حالتي
المضارع أو الماضي. والصفة (the adjective) لا تجمع وتستعمل للمذكر والمؤنث على حد سواء.

Example:	مثال:
A poor boy.	ولد فقير
Poor boys	أولاد فقراء
The boy is poor.	الولد فقير
The boys are poor.	الأولاد فقراء
A small girl	بنت صغيرة
The girl is small.	البنت الصغيرة
A big house	بيت كبير
The house is big	البيت كبير
The man is happy	الرجل سعيد
A happy man	رجل سعيد
The happy man	الرجل السعيد
A difficult lesson	درس صعب
An easy lesson	درس سهل

An unhappy man	رجل غير سعيد
The lesson is difficult	الدرس صعب
The lesson was difficult	كان الدرس صعباً
The lesson has been difficult	لقد كان الدرس صعباً
The book is new.	الكتاب جديد
I bought a new book today	اشتريت كتاباً جديداً اليوم
Ali has a new bicycle.	علي عنده دراجة جديدة
Yousef has an old bicycle.	يوسف عنده دراجة قديمة
He has a bad dog.	عنده كلب رديء/شرير
The garden is waterless.	الحديقة جافة/بدون ماء
The man has a new nectie.	الرجل عنده ربطة عنق جديدة
unhappy	غير سعيد
uneducated	غير مثقف
uneasy	صعب/مرتبك/متقلقل
unsettled	غير مفصول فيه/غير مستقر
Unemployed	غير مُسْتَخدَم/عاطل عن العمل
He made an unhappy trip.	قام بسفرة غير سعيدة
He is an uneducated man.	هو رجل غير مثقف
It is an uneasy job.	إنها مهمة/عمل غير سهل
It is an unsettled question.	إنه أمر غير مفصول فيه/متنازع فيه

ملاحظة: تتمثل الصفة البسيطة (positive degree) في صيغتها أي مجردة/منفردة، مثل: ولد حسن/ جيد

a (good) boy

وكذلك تستعمل للمعادلة والمساواة وذلك بوضع الصفة البسيطة وسط (as...as) وتعني (مثل) فنقول مثلاً:

This boy is (as good as) that boy.

هذا الولد جيد مثل ذاك الولد

Ali is (nice)

علي لطيف/ودود

Yousef is (as nice as) Ali.

يوسف لطيف مثل علي

وتستعمل لنفي المساواة أو المعادلة (so.... as) وتعني (ليس كذلك/ليس مثل). هذا الولد ليس جيداً/حسناً مثل ذاك الولد.

The boy is not (so good as) that boy.

Yousef is not (so nice as) Ali.

يوسف ليس لطيفاً مثل علي.

The boys are (nice).

الأولاد مهذبون.

These boys are (as nice as) those in the class.

هؤلاء الأولاد مهذبون مثل أولئك الذين في الفصل.

Those boys are not so nice as those in the class.

هؤلاء الأولاد ليسوا مهذبين مثل أولئك الذين في الفصل.

Amira is tall.

أميرة طويلة.

Amira is (as tall as) layla.

أميرة طويلة مثل ليلى.

Layla is (not tall as) Amira.

ليلى ليست طويلة مثل أميرة.

وتتكون صفة التفضيل (المقارنة) وذلك بإضافة (er) إلى الصفة البسيطة مع استعمال كلمة (than) وتعني (من) (حرف عطف) وتأتي بعد الصفة مباشرة.

Example:

مثل:

Amira is old.

- الصفة البسيطة – أميرة مُسِنَّة

125

Amira is (older) than layla.

أميرة أكبر سنًّا من ليلى – صيغة التفضيل

Layla is (not so older) than Amira.

ليلى ليست أكبر سنًّا من أميرة.

كما يلاحظ هنا وجود صفات شاذة عن القواعد التي ذكرت آنفاً.

Irregular Comparisons:

صيغة التفضيل الشاذة:

big	كبير	bigger than	أكبر من
good	حسن/جيد	better than	أحسن من
bad	رديء/سيء	worse than	أردأ/أسوأ من
little	قليل/صغير	less than	أقل من
much	كثير (للكمية)	more than	أكثر من (للكمية)
many	كثير (للعدد)	more than	أكثر من (للعدد)

أما بشأن صفة التفضيل العليا (superlative degree) فإنها تتكون بإضافة (est) إلى الصفة البسيطة المجردة أي إلى (positive degree) ويستعمل معها حرف الجر (of) ويعني (من).

مثل: لاحظ لا بد من وضع كلمة (than) في الخانة (2)   Example:

Positive		Comparative		Superlative	
big	كبير	bigger than	أكبر من	biggest of	الأكبر من
hot	ساخن	hotter than	أكثر سخونة من	hottest	الأكثر سخونة من
nice	لطيف	nicer	ألطف من	nicest	الألطف
long	طويل	longer	أطول من	longest	الأطول
tall	طويل	taller	أطول من	tallest	الأطول
pretty	لطيف	prettier	ألطف من	prettiest	الألطف
old	قديم	older	أقدم من	oldest	الأقدم

ملاحظة هامة: تُستعمل (more than) للمقارنة و(most of) للتفضيل العليا وخاصة للصفات المكونة من

أكثر من مقطع (أي الصفات الطويلة) مثل:

Positive 1		Comparative 2	Superlative 3
dangerous	خطير	more dangerous	most dangerous of
beautiful	جميل	more beautiful	most beautiful of
useful	مفيد	more useful	most useful of
difficult	صعب	more difficult	most difficult of
unsettled	غير مستقر	more unsettled	most unsettled of
economical	اقتصادي	more economical	most economical
troublesome	مزعج	more troublesome	most troublesome
interesting	مشوق	more interesting	most interesting

Synonym (مرادف)		Antonym (مناقض)	
knowledgeable	حسن الاطلاع	ignorant	جاهل
light	ضوء/نور	dark	ظلام/مظلم
clean	نظيف	dirty	قذر/وسخ
rich	غني	poor	فقير
easy	سهل	difficult	صعب
happy	سعيد	unhappy	تعيس/حزين
beautiful	جميل	ugly	قبيح
cheap	رخيص	dear	غال/ثمن غالي
famous	شهير/ممتاز	infamous	سيء السمعة
true	حقيقي	false	زائف/خاطئ
right	صحيح	wrong	خطأ
cheap	رخيص	expensive	غال الثمن
right	يمين	left	يسار
generous	كريم	greedy	جشع/طماع
powerful	قوي/جبار	powerless	غير قوي/ضعيف
strong	قوي	feeble	ضعيف
delicious	لذيذ/شهي	acrid	قارص/لاذع
sweet	حلو/عذب	bitter	مُر/قارص/مرير
important	مهم	unimportant	غير مهم

Positive		Comparative	Superlative
big	كبير	bigger than	the biggest of ...
hot	ساخن	hotter than	the hottest of ...
deep	عميق	deeper than	the deepest of ...
short	قصير	shorter than	the shortest of ...
low	منخفض	lower than	the lowest of ...
ugly	قبيح	uglier than	the ugliest of ...
light	خفيف	lighter than	the lightest of ...
quick	سريع	quicker than	the quickest of ...
strong	قوي	stronger than	the strongest of ...
cheap	رخيص	cheaper than	the cheapest of ...
dear	غال	dearer than	the dearest of ...
wide	واسع	wider than	the widest of ...
heavy	ثقيل	heavier than	the heaviest ...
hard	صعب	harder than	the hardest of ...
slow	بطيء	slower than	the slowest of ...
angry	غضبان	angrier than	the angriest of ...
tall	طويل	taller than	the tallest of ...
small	صغير	smaller than	the smallest of ...
clever	ذكي	cleverer than	the cleverest of ...
cold	بارد	colder than	the coldest of ...

weak	ضعيف	weaker than	the weakest of …
smooth	ناعم	smother than	the smoothest of ..
expensive	غال الثمن	more expensive	most expensive
dangerous	خطير	more dangerous	most dangerous
beautiful	جميل	more beautiful	most beautiful
comfortable	مريح	more comfortable	most comfortable
interesting	مهم/مشوّق	more interesting	most interesting
obstinate	عنيد/مستعص	more obstinate	most obstinate
well-off	حسن الأحوال	more well-off	most well-off
shallow	ضحل/سطحي	more shallow	most shallow
intelligent	ذكي/بارع	more intelligent	most intelligent
economical	اقتصادي	more economical	most economical
troublesome	مزعج	more troublesome	most troublesome
useful	مفيد	more useful	most useful
important	مهم/هام	more important	most important
splendid	رائع/ممتاز	more splendid	most splendid

Irregular Adjectives: الصفات الشاذة:

good	حسن/جيد	better than	أحسن	best of	الأحسن
bad	رديء	worse than	أردأ	worst of	الأردأ
little	قليل	less than	أقل	least of	الأقل
far	بعيد	farther than	أبعد	farthest of	الأبعد
far	طويل	further than	مسافة أبعد	furthest of	أشد بعداً
few	قليل	fewer than	أقل	the fewest	الأقل
much	كثير	more than	أكثر	most of	الأكثر

Exercise (17):

(a) Give the comparative

and the superlative of the

following adjectives. eg:

تمرين (17):

اجعل من الصفات التالية

مرة في حالة المقارنة ومرة

أخرى في حالة التفضيل العليا مثل:

Positive	Comparative	Superlative
1- good	better than	the best of
2- beautiful		
3- little		
4- difficult		
5- many		
6- dangerous		
7- nice		
8- wide		
9- useful		

10- strong		
11- happy		
12- bad		
13- greedy		
14- far		
15- much		
16- expensive		
17- old		

ملاحظة: عكس (somebody) هو (nobody) وعكس (something) هـو (anything) يستعمل بـشأن

التفضيل العليا أداة التعريف (the) مثل: (The best of all).

(b) Put the following sentences into: ضع الجمل الآتية في:

Negative	نفي	Interrogative	سؤال

1- I have some books at home.

1- ....

2- He has some money with me.

2- ....

3- There are some dogs in the field.

3- ....

4- I have some work today.

4- ....

5- They can do something for me.

5- ....

6- She told to somebody the story.

6- ....

7- Someone has taken the book.

7- ....

8- I want some news today.

8- ....

9- There is somebody here.

9- ....

10- We want to read some books.

10- ....

Lesson Twenty Six	الدرس السادس والعشرون

الظرف

Adverbs

تأتي الظروف وهي متنوعة في الزمان والمكان وفي السلوك أو الحالة بعد الفعل أو في آخر الجملة. وتعتبر صياغة الظروف الإنجليزية مرنة في وضعها ولكن فيما يخص ظروف الزمان يُستحسن أن تكون في بداية الجملة إذا كانت تحتوي على أكثر من ظرف.

Kinds of Adverbs:	**أنواع الظروف:**
(a) Adverbs of Time	**(أ) ظروف الزمان**
1- Tomorrow	غداً – (الغد)
2- Today	اليوم
3- Yesterday	أمس/البارحة
4- The day after tomorrow	بعد غد
5- The day before yesterday	أمس الأول
6- Tonight – This evening	الليلة/هذا المساء
7- This morning	هذا الصباح
10- now	الآن
11- then	آنئذٍ/أنذاك/بعدئذ/ثم
12- afterwards	بعد ذلك/بعدئذ/في ما بعد
13- before	قبل/من قبل/سابقاً

14- early	في وقت مبكر/مبكراً
15- yet	فوق ذلك/حتى الآن/بل و...
16- still	لا يزال/ومع ذلك/حتى الآن
17- on time – in time	في الوقت المحدد
18- often	كثيراً ما/ في أحوال كثيرة
19- soon	قريباً/عاجلاً/باكراً
20- late	متأخراً/متأخر
21- until now	حتى الآن
22- so far	حتى الآن/إلى هذا الحد
23- lately	مؤخراً

(b) Adverbs of Place: (ب) ظروف المكان

1- far	بعيد
2- near	قريب
3- here and there	هنا وهناك
4- where?	أين؟
5- elsewhere	في مكان آخر
6- everywhere	في كل مكان
7- inside-within	داخل/ضمن- من الداخل
8- outside – without	الخارجي من/خارجاً – خارج كذا
9- behind	وراء
10- in front of – before	أمام

11- backward	خلف
12- forward	أمام
(c) Adverbs of Manner-Quality:	**(ج) ظروف السلوك أو الحالة:**
1- well	حسناً/راضي/مستحسن
2- worse	أسوأ/في حالة أسوأ
3- also	أيضاً
4- too	أيضاً
5- in vain	عبثاً
6- otherwise	وإلّا/بطريقة أخرى/أحياناً
7- badly	على نحو رديء/على نحو خطير
8- better	أحسن
9- thus	هكذا
10- as	مثل/بينما/ في الوقت الذي
11- like	مثل
12- together	معاً
13- also-too	أيضاً/أيضاً

ملاحظة: بالإضافة إلى أنواع الظروف المذكورة توجد أنواع أخرى مثل:

Adverbs of quantity

الظروف الخاصة بالكمية

too much	كثير جداً	much		كثير
nearly	تقريباً	enough		كافي
only	فقط	almost		تقريباً
less	أقل	little		قليلاً

Adverbs of Affirmative and negative

الظروف للإثبات والنفي

Yes – no – not – nothing – anything – really (حقيقة)

وهناك أنواع من الظروف تشتق من الصفة مثل:

final	نهائي	finally	على نحو نهائي
quick	سريع	quickly	بسرعة
especial	خاص	especially	بشكل خاص

Example:

مثال:

1- I shall go to the game tomorrow.

سوف أذهب إلى المباراة غداً.

2- My birthday is today.

عيد ميلادي اليوم.

3- I sold my car yesterday.

بعت سيارتي يوم أمس.

4- The President will talk the day after tomorrow.

سيتحدث الرئيس بعد غدٍ.

5- They came to see me the day before yesterday.

جاءوا ليرَوْني (ليزوروني) أمس الأول.

6- The lesson will be done this

سوف يُعمل الدرس هذا الصباح

morning.

7- He is here now.

هو هنا الآن

8- Now you knew that was wrong.

الآن عرفت أنه غلط

9- Now what do you mean?

والآن ماذا تقصد؟

10- Now and then he comes here.

أحياناً/ من حين إلى آخر يأتي هنا

11- First comes spring; then summer.

يأتي أولاً الربيع ثم الصيف.

12- The house was small at first, but afterwards it became a large house.

كان المنزل صغيراً أول الأمر ولكن بعد ذلك صار منزلاً كبيراً.

13- The lesson starts in the morning very early.

يبدأ الدرس في الصباح في وقت مبكر جداً.

14- Don't go yet.

لا تذهب بعد.

15- It is yet light.

لا يزال هناك ضوء.

16- You can read still better if you will try.

لا تزال تستطيع أن تقرأ أحسن لو تجرب/لو تحاول.

17- He is still busy.

لا يزال مشغولاً.

18- It is still raining, we must go shopping.

لا زالت تمطر، نحن يجب أن نذهب لنتسوق.

19- We arrived at the school in time.

وصلنا إلى المدرسة في الوقت المحدد

20- He bought a new car on time.

اشترى سيارة جديدة في الوقت المحدد

21- We often go to the playing field.

كثيراً ما نذهب إلى أرض الملعب.

22- How often do you go to the super-market?

كم مرة تذهب إلى مجمع الأسواق؟

23- Blame is often directed towards the wrong person.

في أحوال كثيرة يكون اللوم موجه إلى الشخص الخاطئ (المذنب).

24- I will see you again soon.

سأراك مرة ثانية قريباً/عاجلاً.

25- You are very late to school.

جئت متأخراً جداً للمدرسة.

26- He will not be here until tomorrow.

سوف لا يكون هنا حتى/ إلى الغد

27- Winter came last year ultimately.

جاء الشتاء السنة الماضية قبل أوانه/في غير أوانه.

28- So far she has not any knowledge.

إلى هذا الحد لا تعرف أي شيء – إلى هذا الحد ليس لديها أي علم/معرفة.

29- He has not been well lately.

لم يكن في حال حسنة مؤخراً.

30- We don't live far.

لا نسكن بعيداً.

31- We are near here.

نحن نسكن قريباً هنا.

32- He comes from there too.

هو قادم من هناك أيضاً.

33- Sit there!

اجلس هناك!

34- Sit here!

اجلس هنا!

35- You are mistaken there.

أنت غلطان في هذه النقطة.

36- My friend here can help you.

صديقي هذا يستطيع أن يساعدك.

37- Where is the harm in trying to see him?

أين الضرر في أن تحاول أن تراه؟

38- Please step inside here.	من فضلك/ أرجوك أن تخطو داخلاً هنا.
39- Please step outside there.	من فضلك/أرجوك أن تخطو خارجاً هناك.
40- Stand behind me, please.	قِفْ ورائي، من فضلك.
41- The class is behind in its work.	الفصل متأخر في عمله.
42- My house is in front the school.	منزلي أمام المدرسة.
43- The world seems to go backward.	يظهر أن العالم يذهب إلى الخلف / إلى الوراء.
44- He brought forward new several ideas.	جـاء بأفكـار (آراء) جديـدة منطلقـة إلى الأمـام (متقدمة).
45- He is well today.	هو جيد اليوم/ هو في حالة جيدة اليوم.
46- He is worse today.	هو في حالة أسوأ اليوم.
47- That book is useful and cheap also.	ذلك الكتاب مفيد ورخيص أيضاً.
48- We, too are going away.	نحن أيضاً سنذهب/سنخرج.
49- He ate too much. He became ill.	أكل كثيراً فصار مريضاً.
50- I am too glad to help you.	إني(جد) مسرور لمساعدتك.
51- The summer passed too quickly.	الصيف مرَّ بسرعة جداً.
52- He passed the winter in Beirut.	قضى فصل الشتاء في مدينة بيروت.
53- The injured man shouted in vain for help.	صرخ الرجل المجروح عبثاً

ليساعدوه (صرخ من دون فائدة).

54- I made vain attempts to reach you by telephone.

كانت المحاولات عبثاً للاتصال بك (كانت

المحاولات دون فائدة) عن طريق الهاتف.

55- Come at once, otherwise, you will be late to school.

تعال بسرعة وإلا ستكون متأخراً عن المدرسة.

56- He reads and writes badly.

يقرأ ويكتب على نحو رديء.

57- He drives badly.

يقود بطريقة سيئة

58- You better see the teacher.

من المستحسن أن ترى المدرس.

59- He studied hard; thus he got high marks.

قد درس بجد، وهكذا حصل على درجات عالية.

60- Some animals, as dogs and cats, eat meat.

بعض الحيوانات كالكلاب والقطط تأكل اللحم.

61- Treat others as you wish them to treat you.

عامل الآخرين مثل ما أنت ترغب (منهم) أن

يعاملوك.

62- Layla is like her mother.

ليلى مثل أمها.

63- She can sing like a bird.

تستطيع أن تغني مثل/ كالطير.

64- It looks like rain.

يظهر وكأنه مثل المطر.

65- The king is sick and likely to die.

الملك مريض وربما سيموت.

66- I shall very likely be at home all day.

سأكون من المحتمل جداً في المنزل اليوم كله.

67- The girls were walking together in the class.	كانت البنات يسرن معاً/ بعضهن بعضاً في الفصل.
68- You cannot have day and night together.	لا يمكنك أن تحصل على النهار والليل معاً.
69- He reads for hours together.	يقرأ لعدة ساعات بدون انقطاع.
70- I did not hear much of the talk.	لم أسمع كثيراً من الحديث/ من الكلام.
71- I was much pleased with the toy.	كنت مسروراً جداً باللعبة.
72- Have you played enough?	هل لعبت بكفاية؟
73- I don't earn enough money.	لا أكسب نقوداً كافية.
74- Nothing arrived by mail.	لا شيء وصل بالبريد.
75- Have you anything to eat?	هل يوجد معك شيء للأكل؟
76- Father always has the final word.	أبي له دائماً الكلمة الأخيرة.
77- The lost car has been found finally in the market.	السيارة المفقودة قد وجدت في النهاية في السوق.
78- This book is especially prepared for you.	هذا الكتاب أُعد خصيصاً / بصورة خاصة لك / لكم.

حالة الملكية (المضاف إليه/ حالة الجر)

The Possessive Case

تُستعمل صيغة المضاف إليه في ثلاث حالات مثلاً:

الحالة الأولى: باستعمال (of the) كأداة إضافة وتعني (خاص بـ) مثل:

the book (of the) student.	كتاب الطالب
the door of the house.	بابُ المنزل.
the key of the building.	مفتاحُ المبنى.
the vocabulary of the book.	كلماتُ الكتاب / مفرداتُ الكتاب
the house of the teacher.	منزلُ المُدَرِّس

لاحظ: حذفُ أداة التعريف (the) عندما يتعلق باسم شخص مثل:

The friends (of) Lamya.	أصدقاء لمياء
The book of Ali.	كتاب علي

والحالة الثانية: باستعمال حرف (s') والفاصلة العليا (') قبل الاسم في المفرد وفي حالة التنكير:

Example:	مثال:
a boy's book	كتابُ ولدٍ
a teacher's map	خريطةُ مُعلِّمٍ
a man's watch	ساعةُ رجلٍ
a woman's bag	حقيبةُ امرأةٍ

الحالة الثالثة: باستعمال الفاصلة العليا (') بعد الجمع وفي حالة التنكير مثل:

boys' book	كتابُ أولاد
teachers' house	منزلُ معلمين
The boys' exercise books	كتب تمرينات الأولاد
All people like to drink the cows' milk.	كل الناس يرغبون شرب حليب الأبقار.

ملاحظة: لاحظ مرة أخرى هذه الجملة المتعلق بالمضاف إليه:

1- My friend's house is near my school.	منزل صديقي قريب من مدرستي.
2- Ali's new car is white.	سيارة علي الجديدة بيضاء.
3- The student's book is very old.	كتاب الطالب قديم جداً.
4- The horse' color is brown.	لون الحصان أسمر/ بني.
5- The cat's food is in its small hut.	طعام القطة في كوخها الصغير.

ملاحظة: لا تستعمل صيغة المضاف The possessive case إليه المتكونة بالفاصلة العليا وحرف (s') للأشياء أي (أسماء الأشياء) ولكن تستعمل بدلها أداة الملكية (of the).

Example:	**مثال:**
1- The leg of the table is big.	1- رجل الطاولة كبيرة.
2- The papers of the book are very old.	2- أوراق الكتاب قديمة جداً.
3- The color of the pen is yellow.	3- لون قلم الحبر أصفر.

4- The leaves of tree are green. ‏4- أوراق الشجرة خضراء.‏

‏ولكن هناك بعض الاستثناءات بالنسبة لأسماء الأرض‏ the earth – ‏القمر‏ the moon – ‏الشمس‏ the sun

‏– وكذلك الكلمات التي تتعلق بالزمن – لحظة‏ moment – ‏ساعة‏ hour – ‏أسبوع‏ week – ‏أسبوعين‏

fortnight – ‏شهر‏ month – ‏سنة‏ year – ‏يوم‏ day .

‏وكذلك أسماء مشخصة – مثل: النهر‏ the river – ‏باخرة‏ a ship – ‏حياة‏ life – ‏تستعمل معها الفاصلة‏

‏العليا وحرف‏ (s).

Example: ‏مثال:‏

(1) what is the sun's work? ‏ما هو عمل الشمس؟‏

(2) the moon's brightness is beautiful. ‏سطوع القمر جميل.‏

(3) He wants a year's leave. ‏يريد إجازة سنة.‏

(4) Ali has his month's pay. ‏علي عنده راتبه الشهري.‏

(5) The ship's course brought us near the river's ‏سير الباخرة أوصلنا بالقرب من حدود النهر.‏
banks.

(a) Put these sentences into possessive form.

ضع الجمل التالية في صيغة المضاف إليه:

1- The book of the boy. ....

2- The books of the boys. ....

3- The names of the women. ....

4- The eyes of the cat. ....

5- The advice of the teacher. ....

6- The shop of the tailor. ....

7- The wife of the farmer. ....

8- I want my month's pay. ....

9- The dog's food is bad. ....

Lesson Twenty Eight   الدرس الثامن والعشرون

الضمائر الانعكاسية

The Reflexive Pronouns

تُستعمل الضمائر الانعكاسية (reflexive pronouns) المذكورة أدناه للدلالة على أن فاعل الشيء هو ذاته.

أي أنه باستعمال الضمير الانعكاسي يكون صفة للفعل الذي يكُون مفعوله نفس فاعله. وعني الـذات أو

ذاته.

Example: مثال:

I cut myself with a knife.   جرحت نفسي بالسكين

I wrote the report myself.   كتبت التقرير بنفسي.

Pronouns	Reflexive Pronouns		الضمائر الانعكاسية:
I	myself	نفسي	أنا
you	yourself	نفسكَ / نفسكِ	أنتَ/ أنتِ
he	himself	نفسه	هو
she	herself	نفسها	هي
it	itself	نفسه/ نفـسها لغـير العاقل	هو/هي
we	ourselves	أنفسنا	نحن
you	yourselves	نفسكم/نفسكنَّ	أنتم / أنتنَّ
they	themselves	أنفسهم/أنفسهنَّ	هؤلاء

كما يُستعمل الضمير الانعكاسي للتأكيد/للتشديد/ للتعبير عن ذاته مثلاً:

1- I hurt myself with the knife.	جرحت نفسي بالسكين.
2- Ask yourself what you want.	اسأل نفسك ماذا تريد.
3- He cut himself with the razor.	جرح نفسه بموسى الحلاقة.
4- He asked himself what he wants.	سأل نفسه ماذا يريد.
5- He kept the money for himself.	احتفظ بالنقود لنفسه.
6- She herself a good cook.	هي نفسها طباخة جيدة.
7- The cat itself took the fish.	القطة نفسها أخذت السمكة.
8- We ourselves will do the work.	نحن بأنفسنا سنعمل العمل.
9- The boys hurt themselves.	الأولاد جرحوا أنفسهم.
10- They themselves told the story.	هم بأنفسهم أخبروا القصة.

ضع صيغة الملكية أو الضمير الانعكاسي في الفراغ:

1- That is not ..... it is .... She bought it ....

2- This is .... It is not .... I bought it ....

3- She drives .... own car .... everyday.

4- I cut .... with an old knife yesterday.

5- We really enjoyed .... very much in your house.

6- You have to do the exercises by ....

7- This bicycle is .... I bought it ....

8- Layla .... gave the exercise to the teacher.

9- You must all look after .... on .... stay abroad.

ضع كلمة (some) أو كلمة (any) في الفراغ:

1- There isn't .... book on the table.

2- Please give me .... more bread.

3- You have .... nice boys at the school.

4- Go and ask for .... more paper.

5- I want .... of these books for myself.

6- Did he give you .... ink?

7- Did she put ..... more sugar in the tea?

8- Have you seen ..... body here?

9- Yes I have seen ...... body here.

10- I lost my money ..... where.

11- I don't know ...... thing.

ضمائر وأدوات الاستفهام الأساسية

Interrogative pronouns

لاحظ أن ضمائر الاستفهام المذكورة أدناه لها قواعد لا بد من مراعاتها بدقة ويطلق عليها باللغة الإنجليزية

(Question words):

Question Words:	أدوات تستعمل للسؤال:
1- Who …..?	تُستعمل للأشخاص وتعني – مَنْ...؟
2- What ….?	تُستعمل للأشياء وتعني – ما/ماذا....؟
3- Where ….?	تُستعمل للمكان وتعني – أين....؟
4- Which …..?	تُستعمل للاختيار وتعني – أي ....؟
5- How ….?	تُستعمل للنمط /للطريقة وتعني – كيف....؟
6- How many ….?	تُستعمل للعدد وتعني – كم...؟
7- How much …..?	تُستعمل للثمن وللكمية وتعني – كم ....؟
8- Whose ……?	تُستعمل للأشخاص وتعني – لِمَنْ ...؟
9- When …. ?	تُستعمل للزمان وتعني – مَتى .... ؟
10- How old ….?	تُستعمل للعمر وتعني – كم....؟
11- Why …..?	11- تُستعمل للسبب وتعني – لماذا ....؟
12- Of whom ….?	12- (عن من؟) وتعني – مَنْ ....؟

13- Whom ....?   13- تُستعمل للأشخاص وتعني – من ....؟

14- Which of .....?   تُستعمل للاختيار وتعني – أي .....؟

كما ويلاحظ أيضاً أن بعد أداة الاستفهام (how - why - where - when) تكون الجملة في حالة استفهام

أي أن يأتي الفعل قبل الفاعل مثل:

1- When (are) you going?	4- How (did) it happen?
2- Where (is) my book?	5- How (did) you write this?
3- Why (are) you late?	6- Where (is) your new car?

ولاحظ أيضاً استعمال ضمائر أو أدوات الاستفهام التالية ومكانة الفعل:

1- Who goes there?   من يسير هناك؟

2- Who is your friend?   من هو صديقك؟

3- What is wrong with this clock?   ماذا بها الساعة؟

4- What do you want?   ماذا تريد؟

5- What is your opinion on this lesson?   ما رأيك بهذا الدرس؟

6- Where do you live?   أين تسكن؟

7- Where did you put the book?   أين وضعت الكتاب؟

8- Where do you come from?   من أي بلد أنت؟

9-Which books are yours?   أي كُتُبٍ لك؟

10- How did it happen?   كيف حدث هذا؟

11- How many times did you go there?   كم مرة ذهبت هناك؟

12- How many children do you have?   كم عدد أطفالك؟

13- How much is the admission?	كم ثمن الدخول؟
14- How much milk do you want in the tea?	كم تريد حليب بالشاي؟
15- Whose book is this?	كتاب من هذا؟
16- Whose is this book?	لمن هذا الكتاب
17- Whose horse did the thief steal	حصان من الذي سرقه السارق؟
18- When does the school close?	متى تقفل المدرسة؟
19- When do you want to go to Paris?	متى تريد أن تذهب إلى باريس؟
20- How old are you?	كم عمرك؟
21- How old is he?	كمر عمره؟
22- Ho old is this child?	كم عمر هذا الطفل؟
23- Why are you late this morning?	لماذا تأخرت هذا الصباح
24- Why! Why! Are you lazy?	لماذا ولماذا أنت كسول؟
25- With whom are you talking?	مع من تتحدث؟
26- To whom are you giving this book?	لمن تُعطي هذا الكتاب؟
27- Which door was open today?	أي باب كان مفتوحاً اليوم؟

Lesson Thirty	الدرس الثلاثون

الأسماء الموصولة

Relative Pronouns

Relative Pronouns:	الأسماء الموصولة واستعمالاتها:
1- Who	الذي – اللذان – اللذين – الذين للمذكر
2- Who	التي – اللتان – اللتين – اللواتي للمؤنث
Example:	مثال:
The man who was here does not speak the Arabic language.	الرجل الذي كان هنا لا يتكلم اللغة العربية
The woman who was here does not speak the Arabic language.	المرأة التي كانت هنا لا تتكلم اللغة العربية

لاحظ أن الأسماء الموصولة يمكن أن تستعمل على النحو التالي:

Who	الذي/ مفرد وفي حالة الفاعل – مذكر – يستعمل للإنسان
Who	التي/ مفرد وفي حالة الفاعل – مؤنث – يستعمل للإنسان
Who	اللذان/مثنى وفي حالة الفاعل – مذكر – يستعمل للإنسان
Who	التان/ مثنى وفي حالة الفاعل – مؤنث – يستعمل للإنسان
Whom	الذي/ التي/ اللذان/ الذين/ اللواتي يستعمل في حالة المفعول
Which	الذي/ التي/ اللذان/ اللذين/ اللواتي يستعمل للأشياء

157

that	الذي/ التي/ اللذان/ اللتان/ الذين/ اللواتي. في الإمكان استعماله بدلاً من who /whom
	و which وليس كبديل للملكية (whose)

The man who was here does not speak Arabic.

The man **that** was here does not speak Arabic.

The woman **that** was here does not speak Arabic.

My friend, whom you saw, is in the class now.

My friend, **that** you saw, is in the class now.

When	متى/ تستعمل لتدل على الزمن/ الوقت
Whose	لمن/ تستعمل لتدل على الملكية – للانسان فقط
What	ما/ ماذا
Why	لماذا/ للسبب/ بسبب
Of which	لمن/ تستعمل لتدل على الملكية الخاصة بالأشياء فقط

Example:　مثال:

1- The room in which we are now is clean and nice. الغرفة التي نحن فيها الآن نظيفة ولطيفة.

2- The person with whom I was speaking knows my father. الشخص الذي كنت أتكلم معه يعرف والدي.

3- The garden which is round this building is very wide. الحديقة التي حول هذه البناية واسعة جداً.

4- The employee who works in this الموظف الذي يعمل في هذا المكتب غائب

office is absent today.

5- The teacher whom Ali greeted teaches in this school.

المعلم الذي سلم عليه علي يُدَرِّس في هذه المدرسة.

اليوم.

Exercise (20):

تمرين (20):

(a) Put the correct question word in the blank space:

(أ) ضع أداة السؤال المناسبة في المكان الفارغ:

1- .... went with you to Tunisia?

2- .... of these books is the best?

3- .... is my place in this class?

4- .... bus goes to Tripoli?

5- .... is wrong with the clock?

6- .... is your friend's name?

7- .... is the nearest way to the station?

8- .... is the matter?

9- .... of these students is your brother?

10- .... hat is this, mine or yours?

b) Put the correct Relative Pronoun in the blank space:

(ب) ضع الإسم الموصول المناسب في المكان الفارغ:

1- The book .... I was reading yesterday was good.

2- The man .... you spoke to is my son.

3- Where is there a shop .... sells good pictures?

4- I don't like the house .... you saw yesterday.

Lesson Thirty One

الدرس الواحد والثلاثون

كيف تُكَون الأسئلة

How to Form Questions?

إن قبل الشروع في هذا الدرس الجديد يُنصح مراجعة الدرس الخاص بأدوات الاستفهام أو ضمائر الاستفهام المختلفة لأجل معرفة كيفية تكوين السؤال المطلوب في الجمل الاخبارية (statement) المبينـة في التمرينات التالية:

Exercise (21):

تمريـــن(21):

Ask a question for the words in brackets.

ضع سؤالاً للكلمة أو للكلمات بين قوسين

1- (**Ali**) has a new bicycle...   ?

2- (**I**) have been in the school..   ?

3- Ahmed has drunk (**some milk**) ….....................................   ?

4- They went to see (**the teacher**) ……………………......……   ?

5- My name is (**Layla**)……………………….....……………   ?

6- That man is (**my father**) …………………………....……?

7- (**Someone**) has read my letter ……………………....……   ..?

8- We saw (**your brother**) yesterday……………………......   ?

9- I want (**her car**) today………………………………….   ?

10- (**Lamya**) ate the cake ……………………………….   ?

11- We were (**in the school**) today ....?

12- I had (**a bad cold**) last week ....?

13- I am (**twelve years old**) today ....?

14- The sun was (**very hot**) yesterday ....?

15- Ahmed is (**ten years**) old today ....?

Example:

Question and Answer

مثال:

سؤال وجواب

1-   Q. Who is your father?

   A. My father is the owner of this bus.

2-   Q. What is this?

   A. This is a box. (a book – a picture – a new car)

3-   Q. What did you eat today?

   A. I ate some meat today. (drink – drank – milk)

4-   Q. Where are you going tonight?

   A. I am going to see a picture tonight.

5-   Q. How old are you?

   A. I am (18) eighteen years old.

6-   Q. Which kind of books do you want?

   A. I prefer this kind of books.

7-   Q. How is your health today?

   A. Thank you, I am all right. (alright)

8-   Q. How many children have you?

A. I have six children.

9- Q. Whose house is this?

A. It is my father's house.

10- Q. When does this shop open?

A. It opens at five o'clock in the afternoon.

11- Q. How are you?

A. I am well, thank you.

Question-Tag.

What is a question-tag?

عبارة توضع بعد الجملة كقولك (أليس كذلك؟)

<u>ملاحظة</u>: عندما يتحدث الإنجليزي يستعمل في حديثه عبارة للسؤال.. وهـي مقتبسة مـن نفـس الجملـة سواء أكانت في حالة إثبات أو في حالة نفي وذلك لغرض الحصول على الجواب. وهذه العبارة المختصرة مستعملة في جميع اللغـات مثـل: (أليس كـذلك). فـإذا كانت الجملـة المستعملة مـثلاً في حالة إثبـات affirmative sentence تلاحقها (عبارة نفي) وأما إذا كانت الجملة في حالة نفي فتلاحقها (عبارة إثبات)

For Example:

1- You are a teacher, aren't you?

أنت مدرس أليس كذلك

2- You are not a teacher, are you?

أنت لست مدرساً، أليس كذلك؟

مثلما في الجمل التالية:

إذن يتكون الجواب على السؤالين المذكورين أعلاه حسب الظروف سواء كانت بالإيجاب أو بالنفي مثل:

Example:	مثال

1- You are a teacher, aren't you?	أنت مدرس، أليس كذلك
Yes, I am a teacher.	أجل، أنا مدرس
2- You are not a teacher, are you?	أنت لست مدرساً، أليس كذلك؟
No, I am not a teacher, I am a driver of a train.	لا، لست مدرساً، أنا سائق قطار.

لاحظ أن العبارة التي استعملت في حالتي النفي والإثبات والتي تعني (أليس كذلك) باللغة العربية، تحتاج إلى اهتمام خاص لأنها كثيرة الاستعمال لدى الانجليز.

Exercise (22):	تمريـن (22):

Read the sentence and then add the appropriate Question-tag.

اقرأ الجملة ثم أضف عليها عبارة السؤال أو الاستفهام المناسبة أمام الجملة مباشرة.

Question-tag.

1- He is a doctor, ………………………………………… ?

2- He is not a doctor, ……………………………………… .?

3- He isn't a teacher,………………………………………… ?

4- They can do the job, ……………………………………... ?

5- They cannot do the job,…………………………………?

6- She has a beautiful car, ………………………………… ?

7- She has not a beautiful car, …………………………… ?

8- He must write his name clearly, ……………………… ?

9- You are coming soon, …………………………………… ?

10- You are not coming soon, ……………………………… ?

11- We have seen it, ………………………………………….. ?

12- We have not seen it, ……………………………………. ?

13- He is Lebanese, ………………………………………… ?

14- You understand the lesson, ………………………….... ?

15- You'll tell us the story, ………………………………….. ?

16- They can explain this lesson, …………………….......... ?

17- He came by train to school,…………………………….… ?

18- They can have another book, …………………………... ?

19- I wrote a long letter last night, ………………………….. ?

20- She is wearing a new dress, ………………………….….. ?

Questions and Answers:

1   - Did he promise to go with you?

     - Yes, he promised to go with me.

2   - Who went to school with your brother?

     - His friend Ahmed went with my brother.

3   - When did they arrive at the school?

     - They arrived about 6 o'clock at the school.

4   - What does the teacher say about your lesson?

     - He says that I must read too much.

5   - Did you like to read too much?

     - Yes, I do.

6   - Do you like to speak English?

     - Yes, I do.

7   - Do you like to study other languages.

- No, I do not like to study other than this language for the time being.(في الوقت الحاضر)

8   - Can you ask this question in English.

    - Yes, I can.

9   - What is the price of this dinner?

    - It is said that the price is one pound.

10   - How many times do you eat?

    - I eat three times a day.

11   - What are they?

    - They are breakfast, lunch and dinner.

أنواع الجمل Lesson Thirty Two	الدرس الثاني والثلاثون

في اللغة الانكليزية

Types of sentences in English

Three types of sentences in English:

There are three types of sentences in the English language.

They are as follows:

توجد ثلاثة أنواع من الجمل في اللغة الانجليزية من حيث تركيبها وهي على النحو الآتي:

a- The Simple Sentence.

1- الجملة البسيطة (المنفردة).

b- The Compound Sentence.

2- الجملة المركبة (جملتين).

c- The Complex Sentence.

3- الجملة المعقدة (جملتين احدهما أهم من الأخرى).

Explanation:

الشرح:

تتكون الجملة البسيطة (the simple sentence) من فعل واحد. أي أنها تتكون من (مبتدأ + فعل + خبر) فقط.

Example:

مثل:

Ali wrote a book.   We like apples

She read the story.	She teaches Arabic.
I dug a hole.	They know the story.
You drew the cheque	The man cleans the car.
She drinks water.	You opened the door.
He wants a telephone.	I know my lesson.

تتكون الجملة المركبة (Compound) من جملتين منفصلتين محتويتين على فعلين مرتبطتين بحرف عطف

مثل:

1- You can come (and) go in the car.	(و).
2- You can go (but) you must come early.	(ولكن).
3- Is it sweet (or) sour?	(أو)
4- Either eat this (or) go hungry?	(أو)
5- Hurry, (or) you will be late.	(وإلا)
6- The work is not (yet) finished	(بعد) لم ينتهي بعد.
7- Don't go (yet).	(بعد) لا تذهب بعد.
8- The work is good, (yet) it could be better.	(مع ذلك)
9- The chair is broken and has been (so) for a long time.	(هكذا)
10- She is sick. Is that (so?)	(إلى هذا الحد)
11- Ali is here and (so) is Mustafa.	(وكذلك)
12- I said I would go and (so) I shall	(ولذلك)

These are some conjunctions for the compound sentences:

فيما يلي بعض حروف العطف الخاصة بالجمل المركبة .

168

1- and	(و) حرف عطف
2- besides	بالإضافة إلى/ فوق ذلك/ عدا/ علاوة على
3- also	أيضاً/ كذلك
4- further	أيضاً/ علاوة على ذلك
5- moreover	علاوة على ذلك/ فضلاً عن ذلك
6- otherwise	بطريقة أخرى/ وإلا
7- however	على كل حال/ كيفما/ ولكن/ من ناحية أخرى
8- but	ولكن/ لولا أن/ إلا أن/ فحسب فقط
9- still	لا يزال/ ومع ذلك/ حتى الآن
10- nevertheless	ومع ذلك/ وبرغم ذلك
11- consequently	بناء على ذلك/ وهكذا/ وإذن
12- accordingly	وفقاً لذلك/ وهكذا/ وعلى ذلك/ إذن

The Complex Sentence: الجملة المعقدة:

بعد أن شرحنا الجملتين (البسيطة والمركبة) وعرفنا تركيباتهما، نأتي الآن لنشرح الجملة المعقدة. تتكون هذه الصيغة (The Complex Sentence) من جملتين أحدهما أهم من الاخرى بمعنى آخر أن الجملة المعقدة تحتوي على جملة أساسية وجملة تابعة لها ويتم ربطهما بواسطة اسم موصول خاص بهما.

Principal Clause: الجملة الرئيسية:

Subordinate Clause: الجملة التابعة لها:

لا بد أن الدارس قد لاحظ أن مهمة الروابط على اختلاف وظائفها ربط جملتين أحداهما رئيسية والأخرى خاصة بها.

نعطي أدناه جملتين منفصلتين تخصان شخصاً واحداً.

Example: **مثـل:**

(a)   The man does not speak Arabic. (The man) was here.

وبما أن الجملتين تخصان إنساناً فنستعمل الاسم الموصول (who) لربطهما.

(b)   The man (who) was here does not speak Arabic.

لقد حذفنا كلمة (The man) وهي كلمة متكررة واستعملنا بدلها (who) لربط الجملتين. وهكـذا وضعنا

الاسم الموصول (who) كما قلنا مباشرة بعد كلمة (The man). وبهذا صارت الجملة كاملة.

Complex Sentence   وهنا مثال آخر للجملة المعقدة

1-   (a) This is my son. My son is a professor.

      (b) This is my son (who) is a professor.

2-   (a) The teacher teaches in this school. Ali greeted him.

      (b) The teacher (whom) Ali greeted teaches in this school.

لاحظ: لقد استعمل الإسم الموصول (whom) بدلاً من الضمير (him) في حالة المفعـول بـه أي إنـه اسـتعمل

(whom) في مكان المفعول به بعد حذفه من الجملة الأولى. أنظر حرف (b) في الجملة الثانية.

The teacher teaches in this school.   هذه جملة رئيسية

Ali greeted (him).   وهذه جملة تابعة

وقد تم حذف المفعول به (him) بدلاً من تكرار (the teacher).

لاحظ أن الإسم الموصول (whose) يستعمل للملكية للعاقل فقط. انظر استعمال الأسماء الموصولة بـشأن الجملة الرئيسية والتابعة لها.

Example:

مثال:

1- (a) There's the woman

(1) جملة رئيسية

(b) (Her) money has been stolen.

(2) جملة تابعة.

There's the woman (whose) money has been stolen.

2- (a) That is the man

(b) His book was read by many people.

وفي إمكان الدارس أن يستبدل الأسماء الموصولة (which, whom, who) بالإسم الموصول (that) مثل:

(1) The man that was here does not speak Arabic.

(2) My friend that has taken the key is my neighbor

(3) The teacher that Ali greeted teaches in this school.

(4) The professor that you saw yesterday is my son.

(5) This is my school that I go every morning.

(6) Muslims celebrate Eid-El-Fiter that is the end of Ramadan.

Exercise (23):   تمرين (23):

Join the following sentences by a suitable conjunction (till – but – or – and – so – yet – for – until)

أربط الجمل التالية بأدوات الربط المناسبة.

1- He is kind. He is nice.

2- He is a butcher. He does not eat meat.

3- She is ill. She does not go to school.

4- Ali does not eat meat. He is a butcher.

5- Layla does not go to school. She is ill.

6- You can go. You must come early.

7- Is it sweet? Is it sour?

8- The work is good. It could be better.

9- Ali is here. Mustafa is there.

10- Ahmed saw his friend. He was driving a car.

Exercise (24):   تمرين (24):

Join the following sentences by a suitable conjunction. Because – therefore – consequently – otherwise – also – however – still – besides – nevertheless – according to.

كون الجمل التالية بأدوات الربط المناسبة:

1- Boys play football. It is fun.

2- you will be ranked. The work you do.

3- They played all day. They did not go to school.

4- He went to a party. He did not study his lesson.

5- She was very tired. She kept on working.

6- You can read. If you will try.

7- I'll come. I am busy.

8- Come at once. You will be late.

9- I don't want to go playing. It is cold.

10- He didn't want to quarrel. He came to see him.

<table>
<tr><td>**Conjunctions:**</td><td>حروف عطف أخرى</td></tr>
<tr><td>1- either .... or</td><td>إما وإما: للاختيار</td></tr>
<tr><td>2- neither .... nor</td><td>لا ولا</td></tr>
<tr><td>3- therefore ...</td><td>لذلك/ وعليه/ بسبب ذلك/ إذن</td></tr>
<tr><td>4- while ...</td><td>بينما/ مادام</td></tr>
<tr><td>5- although...</td><td>ولو إن: حرف عطف للتناقض/ مع ذلك</td></tr>
<tr><td>6- though...</td><td>مع ذلك/ برغم ذلك/ ولو أن</td></tr>
</table>

لاحظ أن بعد عملية الربط بين جملتين بواسطة أي حرف عطف يتغير الـضمير إلى حـرف صـغير باسـتثناء الضمير (I) وكذلك في أي حرف آخر.

<table>
<tr><td>**Conjunctions:**</td><td>حروف عطف أخرى</td></tr>
<tr><td>1- when ...</td><td>عندما/ بالرغم أن/ في حين</td></tr>
<tr><td>2- if...</td><td>إذا/ ولو أنه/ لو/ ليت</td></tr>
<tr><td>3- whether</td><td>إذا/ أي الاثنين</td></tr>
</table>

173

4- as soon as …	مجرد/ بمجرد
5-after…	بعد: (لاحظ متى يستعمل هذا الحرف)
6- before	قبل: (لاحظ متى يستعمل هذا الحرف)
7- unless	إلا إذا/ إذا لم/ ما

The use of conjunctions.

لاحظ استعمال حروف العطف في جمل مختلفة.

1- Either come in or go out.

2- Ali neither studies nor learns.

3- I think therefore I am.

4- He plays while he must study hard.

5- Although it rained all day, they went on foot.

6- The dog comes when it is called.

7- Come if you can. Come tomorrow if you can.

8- Whether sick or well, he is always cheerful.

9- I'll let you know as soon as I hear the story.

10- I wrote the letter after I had seen my teacher.

11- I had written the letter before I saw the teacher.

12- You will fail unless you work hard.

13- We shall go unless it rains.

14- The door must be either open or shut.

15- If it rains tomorrow, we shall stay home.

الدرس الثالث والثلاثون

المفيدة

Useful phrases

a- How much time have you at your disposal?

كم من الوقت في تصرفك؟

b- I have only two weeks.

لدي فقط أسبوعين.

c- I shall spend only five days in this town..

سوف أمضي فقط خمسة أيام في هذه المدينة

a- Do you have two tickets for the match today?

هل لديك بطاقتين لمباراة اليوم

b- I am sorry all the tickets have been sold.

أنا متأسف جميع البطاقات بيعت.

c- They sold them a week ago.

باعوهم منذ أسبوع مضى.

a- How much money do you intend to spend?

كم من النقود قررت أن تصرف؟

b- I intend to spend ten dinars only.

قررت أن أصرف فقط عشرة دنانير

a- Since when have you known him?

منذ متى عرفته؟

b- I have known him for only three years.

عرفته منذ ثلاث سنوات

a- He wrote a very nice letter to the teacher.	كتب رسالة جميلة جداً للمعلمين
b- It was really a very nice letter.	إنها حقاً رسالة جميلة جدا.
a- Where have you spent your time today?	أين أمضيت وقتك اليوم؟
b- I spent it walking (to and from)	أمضيته في المشي ذهاباً وعوده.
- How did you pass the time there?	كيف أمضيت الوقت هناك؟
- At your will.	متى شئت/ متى ترغب
- So long O! my friend	وداعاً/ إلى اللقاء يا صديقي.
- He is willing to wait here.	مستعد أن ينتظر هنا.
- He swore by God.	أقسم بالله العظيم
- I will see you again soon.	سأراك مرة ثانية قريباً
- As soon as I hear, I shall let you know.	حالما أسمع/ بمجرد أن أسمع سأحيطك علماً
- Treat others as you will them to treat you.	عامل الآخرين مثل ما أنت ترغب/ تريد أن يعاملوك
- in the long run.	في خاتمة المطاف/ في النهاية
He will be here very soon.	سيكون هنا قريباً جداً

لاحظ بعض استعمالات لفعل (do) في المضارع:

Do you speak English? Yes, I do.

176

(1) لإنجاز أو تنفيذ شيء ما في صيغة أمر مثل:

Do your homework well.

(2) تصرف/ فعل/ سلك مثل: (هذا يكفي)

That will do

The students did very well today.

(3) للتأكيد/ يعزم علي/ نية/ يفعل شيء **مثل:**

I do want to go to see the football match.

Do come, please.

Do you like this story?

(4) للسؤال

Do you have an English lesson today?

Yes, I do or yes, I do have.

Whose book is this?

I do not know.

It does not belong to me at all.

Do you belong here? Do you live here?

(5) لإحلال مكان فعل آخر أو لعدم تكرار مرة ثانية مثل (My brother goes where I do): فعـل (do) هنـا هو بديل الفعل(go) حيث لا يصح تكراره في نهاية الجملة التي تعني: أخي يذهب أو يذهب أخـي حيـث أذهب أنا.

Do me a favour, close the door.	اعمل معروف ...
(Do away) with that car	(تخلص من) تلك السيارة
Do it again.	كرر ذلك أو افعله مرة ثانية
I cannot do without this book	لا أستطيع أن أستغني عن هذا الكتاب
Do you want more milk?	هل تريد بعض الحليب؟
No, thank you, this will do.	لا، شكراً هذا يكفي.
God Forbid!	لا قدر الله/ لا سمح الله
If you please.	إذا سمحت/ من فضلك/ أرجوك
God willing	إن شاء الله/ هذه هي مشيئة الله
I look forward to see you soon	أرجو أن أراك قريباً
It is impossible to talk	إنه مستحيل أن تتحدث
Without verbs	من غير/ بدون أفعال
Let's (Let us) do an exercise with some verbs.	دعنا نعمل تمريناً بعض الأفعال.
Let's (Let us) begin with a short story.	لنبدأ بقصة قصيرة
Very good	حسناً جداً
1- It is high time to write my lessons.	حان الأوان/ الوقت لكتابة دروسي

2- He comes here at the (usual) time.

يأتي هنا في الساعة المألوفة/ الاعتيادية

3- He goes to school (on foot).

يذهب إلى المدرسة على الأقدام/ على رجليه

4- I only see him from time to time.

إني أراه فقط من وقت إلى آخر.

5- She reads her newspaper from time to time.

تقرأ صحيفتها بعض الوقت/ من وقت إلى آخر

6- This is my address

هذا هو عنواني

7- How kind you are.

كم أنت لطيف. أو كم أنت كريم.

8- Your lesson is wrong.

درسك خاطئ

9- You are quite right.

عندك حق/ أنت على صواب

10- He reads his book in a quiet room.

يقرأ كتابه في غرفة هادئة

11- Gray is a quiet color

اللون الرمادي لون هادئ

12- Undoubtedly, I am well informed about the subject of today.

من غير شك/ بدون ريب إني على علم حول موضوع اليوم

13- I am curious, what is this?

أتعجب، ما هذا

14- Would you like to drink some orange juice?

هل ترغب/ تحب أن تشرب قليلاً/ بعضاً من عصير البرتقال؟

15- Thank you.

شكراً/ أشكرك

16- I already have some of it

عندي من قبل بعض منه

179

17- Do you need some money for the new books?

هل تحتاج إلى نقود لشراء الكتب الجديدة؟

18- No, I don't need any money for the time being.

لا، لست في حاجة للنقود في الوقت الحاضر

19- Because I have enough money.

لأني عندي كفاية نقود/ أو من النقود.

20- While waiting for us he is writing his lesson.

في أثناء انتظارنا يكتب درسه

21- While doing his homework he is listening to the radio.

في أثناء/ أو بينما يعمل واجب دراسي، يصغي إلى الإذاعة

22- On leaving Tripoli, I intend to go to another town.

في الوقت الذي أغادر طرابلس أنوي الذهاب إلى مدينة أخرى

Advice (اسم)

نصيحة/ ينصح

23- To keep well, follow the doctor's advice.

كي تحافظ على الصحة تتبع/ و أتبع نصيحة الدكتور

Advise (فعل)

ينصح

24- He advised me to keep my money in the bank.

نصحني أن أحافظ على نقودي في المصرف

Advisable (صفة)

سديد/ مناسب/ يُشار به

25- It is not advisable for him to go to school while he is not well/ sick.

من غير المناسب الذهاب إلى المدرسة بينما هو في غير صحة جيدة/ أو مريض

26- We had been advised of the dangers before we began our trip

كنا قد نصحنا من الأخطار قبل أن نبدأ رحلتنا إلى الصحراء

180

to the desert.

27- The teacher answered the children's questions about the new story (which) he had been reading to them.

أجاب المعلم على/ أو المعلمة أسئلة الأطفال عـن/ أو حول القصة الجديدة التي كان قد قرأها.

28- Then the teacher questioned the children about what happened in the story.

ثم سأل المعلم/ المعلمة الأطفال عن/ حول ماذا حدث في القصة

29- A matter is out of the question.

مسألة خارجة عن الموضوع

30- This matter is beyond me.

هذه مسألة فوق فهمي

31- This lesson is beside the question.

هذا الدرس لا صلة له بالموضوع كلية/ إطلاقاً.

32- This is a quick reply to my question.

هذا رد سريع على سؤالي.

33- Try always to reply upon (on) your own efforts.

حاول دائماً أن تعتمد على مجهوداتك.

34- I relied upon your promises.

اعتمدت على وعودك

Pardon me

لم أسمع ما قلت/ أستميحك العذر

I beg your pardon

معذرة/ عفواً

Pardon me.

لا تؤاخذني/ عفواً

Yes.

الرد يكون بالموافقة/ تفضل

Please, come in

تفضل تعال/ تفضل أدخل

Help yourself.

تفضل/ اخدم نفسك بنفسك على المائدة

I am sorry, I don't drink	لا تؤاخذني/ متأسف لا أشرب
I agree with you there.	أتفق معك في ذلك الأمر
Woe worth the day!	لعن الله اليوم
Worth it!	يستحق ذلك الجهد أو العناء
The school is empty today	المدرسة فارغة اليوم
because it is holiday	لأنها عطلة
The school is full because it is a day of examinations.	المدرسة كاملة/ ملآنة لأنه يوم الامتحانات
Don't stand if you are tired, but sit down.	لا تقف إذا كنت متعباً ولكن اجلس/ استرح.
The students stood up to salute the flag in the school.	وقف الطلبة ليحيوا العلم في المدرسة
Hope supports us in trouble.	الأمل يعيننا في المتاعب
The facts support my claim.	الأدلة/ الحقائق تؤيد مطالبي
My teacher is a good supporter of good English.	مدرسي مؤيد/ مساعد حسن لأجل دراسة إنجليزية حسنة.

Trouble يقلق/ يوجع/ يزعج/ عناء/ يهتم/ يثير/ يعكر/ يحرج / مشكلة/ خلل

That unhappy student troubles his companions in the school.	ذلك الطالب غير السعيد يقلق رفاقه في المدرسة.
Don't trouble yourself to read that bad book because it is not worth reading it at all.	لا تحرج نفسك أن تقرأ ذلك الكتاب الرديء لأنه لا يستحق

This man is troubling himself too much.	هذا الرجل يقلق نفسه كثير جداً
This student is tireless.	هذا الطالب لا يعرف التعب والكلل
Enslave	يستعبد
have borne world (The world) as free men	قد ولدوا
" Since when may anyone enslave men whom their mothers have born into this world as free men".	« متى (يمكن لأي واحد) استعبدتم الناس (استعباد الناس) وقد ولدتهم أمهاتهم أحراراً في هذا العالم»

Lesson Thirty Four أقارب العائلة	الدرس الرابع والثلاثون

Family Relatives

Family Relatives

Aunt	عمة أو خالة/ زوجة العم أو الخال
Bride	العروسة
Bridegroom	العريس
Brother	أخ
Brotherhood	الأخُوّة
Cousin	ابن عم/ خال
Cousin	بنت عم/ خال
Child	طفل/ طفلة
Children	أطفال
Childless	ابتر/ لا أولاد له
Daughter	ابنة
Father	أب
Fatherhood	الأبوة
fiancé	الخاطب/ خطيب فلانة
fiancée	المخطوبة/ خطيبة فلان

185

Father-in-law	الحمو/ أبو الزوجة أو الزوج
Fatherless	يتيم الأب
Family relatives	أقارب العائلة
Grandfather	جد/ سلف
Grandmother	جدة/ أم الأب أو الأم
Grandparent	جد/ جدة
Grandniece	حفيد ألأخ أو الأخت
Grandson	حفيد
Granduncle	عم/ خال الأب أو الأم
Grandaunt	عمة/ خالة الأب أو الأم
Grandchild	حفيد/ حفيدة
Granddaughter	حفيدة
Husband	زوج
Mother	أم
Motherhood	الأمومة
Mother-in-law	الحماة/ أم الزوج أو الزوجة
Nephew	ابن الأخ/ الأخت
Niece	ابنة الأخ أو الأخت/ ابنة أخ الزوج أو اخته
Wedding, marriage	زفاف/ اقتران
Wedding-day	يوم الزفاف
Wedding-card	بطاقة الاقتران

Parent	أب/ أم
Parentage	أبوة
Parental	أبوي، والدي/ صفة
Parenthood	أبوة
Sister	اخت
Son	ابن
Sweetheart	حبيب/ حبيبة
Uncle	عم/ خال
Wife	زوجة
Widower/widowhood	أرمل/ الترمل
Wifehood	الزوجية
widow	أرملة

ملاحظة:

1- تأتي كلمة (hood) بعد الاسم مباشرة وهي كلمة لاحقة وتعني (حالة) أو الصفة مثل: – motherhood sisterhood

2- تسبق الاسم (grand) ولها معاني كثيرة منها: كبير مثل مكان كبير (grand place)، خطأ كبير (grand mistake).

3- كلمة (less) تأتي بعد الاسم وتعني: أقل/ أدنى مرتبة/ أصغر/ ناقصاً أو مطروحاً من كذا/ جزء أو مقدار أصغر. وتعني أيضاً بلا/ بدون. تقريبا (more or)

187

less) ومن غير أب (fatherless)، ومع ذلك(non-the-less)، محروم من الأولاد (childless).

Words used in sentences

There is (less) rain in this place.   بمعنى أقل

I want (less) butter in my bread.   أقل

The doctor advised me to eat (less) meat.   أقل

He refused to take (less) than two dollars.   أقل من

That man is homeless   بلا منزل أو بدون منزل

He has (less) exercises (than) me   أقل ... من

Nevertheless – nonetheless   مع ذلك/ برغم ذلك

She was very tired; **nevertheless** she kept on working

She was very tired, **nevertheless** she kept on reading.

None (no one)   لا أحد/ لا شيء/ إطلاقاً/ البتة/ بأية حال

1- We have (none) of that paper left.   لا شيء

2- (None) of these books is important.   لا أحد من هذه

3- (None) has arrived in office.   لا أحد أتى إلى المكتب

4- Our supply is (none) too great.   بأية حال

Too (too small)   بمعنى أيضاً كذلك/ أكثر مما ينبغي: مثلا: (صغير جداً)

Shoes are (too) small for me	الحذاء صغير أكثر مما ينبغي
He is (too) late today.	تأخر جداً (أكثر مما ينبغي)
May I come (too)?	أيضاً
The poor man is hungry, and thirsty (too).	كذلك
We (too) are going away.	أيضاً
My dress is (too) long for you.	فستاني طويل جداً
He ate too much.	أكل الكثير مما ينبغي أكله
He came too late.	أتى متأخراً جداً.

Composition: Birthday party   إنشاء

My dear friend Musa, I wish to inform you that today is my brother's birthday. He is (15) fifteen years old. Therefore, I will go with my father, my four cousins and one of my uncles to the shopping center in town for shopping some nice presents for my small brother, for my family relations and for some guests. It is a very happy occasion indeed.

My mother will invite my three aunts with their six children and my father will also invite my other two uncles. Then both father and mother and my two sisters will, all of them, invite their best friends and some of our neighbours in order that all will come home in the evening to celebrate and enjoy the birthday party of my brother Ali. Then after they all had enjoyed the birthday party, Ahmed's brother received his nice presents from his parents, relatives and the guests.

189

Exercise (25):

تمرين (25):

Answer the following questions about Ahmed's birthday party.

أجب على الأسئلة التالية عن عيد ميلاد أحمد.

1- Why does Ahmed wish to inform Musa?

2- How old is Ahmed's brother?

3- With whom will Ahmed go to the shopping center?

4- How many aunts has Ahmed?

5- How many uncles has Ahmed?

6- How many sisters has he?

7- Who will come to the birthday party?

8- How many children have his aunts?

9- When will they celebrate the birthday?

10- Where will Ahmed's brother receive his presents?

1- ....

2- ....

3- ....

4- ....

5- ....

6- ....

7- ....

8- ....

9- ....

10- ....

Lesson Thirty Five

الدرس الخامس والثلاثون

حوارات (عائلة علي)

Conversation: (Ali's Family)

Conversation: (Ali's family)

Ahmed   :   Where do you live, Ali?

Ali   :   I live in the country with my family.

Ahmed   :   Why do all of you live in the country?

Ali   :   Because, as you know, it is hot in the town in this time of the year.

Ahmed   :   Yes, you are right. To live in town in summer time, is really difficult, specially, in Africa. But remember, Africa is healthier than Europe because of the sun which is rare in Europe.

Ali   :   My family spent three months in the country last year when I was out of the country for medical treatment. But this year we will stay in the country for the whole of summer in order to enjoy the fresh air of the country side.

Ahmed   :   What does your family do when they are in town?

Ali   :   We all like to remain at home in winter time. We, as a matter of fact, enjoy very much to stay home. There is nothing you can see when it rains in the town.

Ahmed	:	What else does your family do at home?
Ali	:	In the evening, for example, mother and father read their newspapers; while my brothers and sisters watch the television, and other either listen to some music or read books.
Ahmed	:	Doesn't any of you go to the pictures?
Ali	:	Yes, some of us do go to the pictures. But they don't always do that. However, we like to invite some of our friends at home.
Ahmed	:	It seems to me that you are rich, aren't you?
Ali	:	Well, to say the truth, we are well off. But we spend a lot of money which, in my opinion, is not fair in these difficult days.
Ahmed	:	It is good to think that it is not fair to spend.

معاني المفردات:

while	بينما
It seems to me	يظهر لي/ يتبين لي/ يخيل لي
Well-off	في حالة مرضية/ وضع مرضي
Well-read	واسع الاطلاع (عن طريق المطالعة)
Well-known	معروف/ مشهور
Well-to-do	غني/ ثري/ موسر
In my opinion	في رأيي/ في اعتقادي
Fair – just	عادل/ قانوني/ صائب/ إنصاف
Fairly	على نحو جميل/ لائق/ ملائم

Uselessly	في غير ذي فائدة/ دون جدوى
save	يقتصد/ المحافظة على/ يدخر

Exercise (26): تمرين (26):

Answer the following questions:

1- Where does Ali live?

2- Why does Ali's family live in the country?

3- What is (rare) in Europe?

4- How long did Ali's family spend in the country?

5- What does Ali's family do at home?

6- What isn't fair in Ali's opinion?

للمجهول

Passive Voice

تُستعمل صيغة المبني للمجهول (Passive voice) عندما يكون الفاعل وضمير الفاعل (the doer) غير معروف أو أريد أن يكون مجهولاً أو لا رغبة في ذكر الفاعل. وعلى هذا الأساس يتطلب من المتحدث التغير من جملة مبنية للمعلوم (Active voice) إلى جملة مبنية للمجهول. ولهذه التركيبة اللغوية قواعد لا بد للدارس أن يستوعبها جيداً.

تتكون تركيبة الجملة البسيطة المبنية للمعلوم (كما هو معروف) من اسم أو ضمير + فعل + مفعول به. (وهذا الأخير قد يكون تارة اسم وتارة أخرى ضمير) مثل:

1- Layla writes a letter.	Layla wrote a letter.
2- She drinks cold water.	She drank cold water.
3- Ali reads the lesson.	Ali read the lesson.
4- He has taken the book.	He had taken the book.
5- The horse draws the car.	The horse drew the car.

(2) ولكي تغير الجمل المذكورة أعلاه إلى صيغة المبني للمجهول لا بد أن تُجرى التغييرات التالية:

فتبدأ أولاً بتحويل المفعول به سواء كان إسماً أم ضميراً ليصبح الفاعل أي المبتدأ وتضع فعل (to be) ثانياً أما الفعل الذي يتغير هو الآخر إلى التصريف الثالث إلى (past participle) مع إضافة حرف الجر (by) الذي يُوضع أمام المفعول به وأحياناً لا لزوم له.

لاحظ كيف تم تحويل الجمل المبنية للمعلوم (Active Voice) إلى جمل مبنية للمجهول(Passive Voice) في الجمل التالية:

1- Layla writes a letter every week.

2- She drinks cold water in summer.

3- Ali reads the lesson in the class.

4- He has taken the book since a week.

5- The horse drew the car in the streets.

Passive Voice:

قد تم تحويل الجمل المذكورة أعلاه إلى مبني للمجهول:

1- A letter	is	written	by	Layla every week.
2- Cold water	is	drunk	by	her in summer
3- The lesson	is	read	by	Ali in the class
4- The book	has been	taken	by	him.
5- The car	was	drawn	by	the horse in the street.
6- A letter	was	written	by	Layla every week.

Exercise (27):

تمرين (27):

Change the following into passive voice.

حَوِّل هذه الجمل المبنية للمعلوم إلى جمل مبنية للمجهول.

1- He eats meat every day in this restaurant.

....

2- She was buying a new car yesterday.

....

3- I teach you written English.

....

4- Ali gave a warm welcome.

....

5- They will show her the new house today.

....

6- The farmers will clean the gardens.

....

7- We have seen three boys near the school

....

8- She writes this exercise well.

....

9- You broke the window.

....

10- He gave his brother a new book.

....

لا تنسى المحافظة على نفس زمن الفعل في الجملة عند تحويلها سواء أكانت في حالة

المبني للمجهول أو في حالة المبني للمعلوم.

Exercise (28):

تمرين (28):

Change the following into active voice

غير الآتي إلى جمل مبنية للمعلوم.

1- The trees were blown down by the wind

....

2- The mouse is caught by the cat.

....

3- The sky was hidden by the clouds.

....

4- He could not be forgiven by me.

....

5- This lesson must not be forgotten by you.

....

6- The lecture is being listened by you all.

....

7- Some important books will be given by me to him.

....

8- The old books had been taken away from the house.

....

9- The lesson could be easily told by him.

....

10- This book will be received by you tomorrow.

....

تعبيرات مفيدةLesson Thirty Seven	الدرس السابع والثلاثون

Useful Phrases

Useful Phrases (1):	تعبيرات مفيدة (1):
1- until tomorrow	حتى الغد/ إلى الغد
2- until later/ it is too late	فيما بعد/ فات الأوان
3- where is?!	أين؟!
4- Here is! Here are!	هنا/ ها هنا
5- and so forth	وهلم جرّاً
6- thanks	شكراً
7- enough	كفاية
8- wonderful	هائل/ عظيم/ عجيب
9- by the way	على فكرة
10- with pleasure	بكل سرور
11- not at all	العفو/ لا شكر على واجب
12- I am sorry	متأسف
13- I am very sorry	متأسف جداً
14- one more	واحد آخر/ مرة أخرى
15- the very idea	الفكرة ذاتها

16- many thanks	شكراً كثيراً/ ألف شكر
17- don't mention it	العفو
18- you are welcome	أهلا وسهلاً
19- that is to say	أي/ يعني/ بكلمة أخرى
20- at your service	في خدمتك
21 in the mean time	في نفس الوقت
22- what is the meaning?	ماذا تعني/ ونعني/ ما القصد

Useful Phrases (2):	**تعبيرات مفيدة (2):**
1- It means…	تعني/ يعني
2- I think so	أعتقد كذلك/ هكذا
3- Please take me to the station. (this address).	تعال معي/ خذني إلى المحطة/إلى هذا العنوان
4- Please wait here a minute.	من فضلك انتظر هنا لحظة
5- Stop here/ there	قف هنا/ هناك/ انتظر
6- all right.	حسناً/ طيب/ سليم
7-that's all right.	موافق/ حسناً جداً/ مُرضٍ
8- nothing is easy today!	لا يوجد شيء سهل اليوم!
9- one time/ once.	مرة واحدة/ ذات مرة
10- one by one.	واحداً فواحداً
11- on time	في الموعد المحدد

12- I want to change this book.	أريد أن أغير هذا الكتاب
13- We want to listen to the lesson.	نريد أن نصغي إلى الدرس
14- What is the teacher saying?	ماذا يقول المدرس؟
15- We all can guess the lesson	نحن كلنا نقدر أن نخمن الدرس
16- Only the teacher can give you the right answer.	المدرس فقط يستطيع أن يعطيك الجواب الصحيح؟
17- Can you explain this lesson?	هل تقدر أن تشرح هذا الدرس؟
18- This is to my taste.	هذا على ذوقي/ على مزاجي
19- from time to time	من وقت إلى آخر
20- sometimes	بعض الوقت/ أحياناً
21- He is familiar with him	هو ملم به/ هو يعرفه

Useful Phrases (3): تعبيرات مفيدة (3):

1- How kind you are!	هذا كرم/ لطف منكم
2- You are quite right.	أنت/ انتم على حق
3- We congratulate you	نهنئك/ تهانينا
4- undoubtedly/ no doubt	من غيرشك/ بدون شك
5- at once	حالاً/ في الحال/ بسرعة
6- you are late early	أنت متأخر/ أنت مبكر
7- Thank you very much for your advice	شكراً/ أشكرك كثيراً على نصيحتك
8- as far as I know	بقدر ما أعلم/ بقدر ما أعرف

9- so far so good	كل شيء حسن حتى الآن
10- I should say so!	أظن كذلك
11- Good heaven!	يا للعجب/ يا الله
12- ahead of time!	قبل الأوان/ متقدماً/ إلى الأمام
13- in good time	في الوقت المناسب
14- Good bye/ bye – bye	استودعكم الله/ مع السلامة
15- God spend!	في أمان الله/ وفقك الله
16- by the way!	والشيء بالشيء يذكر/ على فكرة
17- God willing	مشيئة الله/ إن شاء الله
18- in behalf of	بالنيابة عن/ بدلاً من
19- on behalf of	بالنيابة عن/ لأجل
20- not a bit	بتاتاً/ على الإطلاق
21- wait a bit	انتظر قليلاً
22- Give me a bit of bread	أعطني قطعة من الخبز

Useful Phrases (4):	**تعبيرات مفيدة (4):**
1- bitter enemy	عدو لدود
2- until now	للآن/ حتى الآن
3- in advance	مقدماً
4- acquaintance	معرفة شخصية
5- in the long run	في النهاية/ في خاتمة المطاف

6- Please	إذا سمحت/ من فضلك
7- God forbid!	لا قدّر الله/ لا سمح الله
8- If you please	إذا سمحت/ أرجوك
9- Will you please	أرجوك/ من فضلك
10- I look forward to see you	أرجو أن أراك/ آمل أن أرك
11- a short time	وقت قصير
12- a short life	حياة قصيرة
13- Cut short, please	اختصر من فضلك
14- it is all the same to me	سيان عندي/ على حد سواء عندي
15- in the air	في الهواء
16- at your will	متى شئت/ متى ترغب ذلك
17- So long O! my friend.	وداعاً إلى اللقاء يا صديقي
18- He swore By God	أقسم بالله
19- soon	حالاً/ سريعاً
20- as soon as I hear, I will let you know.	حالما أسمع سأحيطك علماً.
21- most likely	في أغلب الظن/ في أكثر الظن
22- about – in respect of	بشأن

See how each phrase was used in a useful sentence:

أنظر كيف استعملت كل مفردة في جملة مفيدة.

- need (يحتاج)

1- I need you today.

2- I need a new car for my next trip.

203

3- Plants always need water.

4- In the desert their need was fresh water.

5- For need of a nail the shoe was lost.

6- He was a friend in need. (كان صديقاً في وقت الضيق)

7- He did not fail us in our need. (لم يقصر)

8- I have need (must يجب) to go to town.

9- You need not bother. (لا تهتم)

10- There is no need to hurry. (لا لزوم للاستعجال)

Look – يشير إلى – يواجه – يشرف – ينظر – يفحص – يراقب

1- I look after my family. (اعتني)

2- He looks for his close friend. (يبحث)

3- We always look forward to better time. (يتطلع)

4- He like to look in that beautiful shop. (يُزور)

5- The teachers decided to look into the tests. (يفحص)

6- Always look out when you go in the darkness. (احترس)

7- Those two boys look like each other. (يشبه)

8- He took the dictionary to look up for a word. (يبحث)

9- Always try to look ahead. (إلى الأمام)

10- look before you leap. (كن حذراً قبل أن تقفز)

11- My school looks on to a beautiful field. (يطل على)

الدرس الثامن والثلاثون الكلام المباشر والغيرLesson Thirty Eight

مباشر

Direct and Indirect Speech

(a) Direct Speech.

أ) الكلام المباشر

(b) Indirect Speech.

(ب) الكلام غير المباشر

(1) أنظر الملاحظات حول صيغة المبني للمجهول.

(2) أود أن أكرر هنا على دارس القواعد الانجليزية التي حاولت أن أبسطها قدر الإمكان أن يكون على دراية جيدة بكل الأزمنة المشروحة سابقاً لكي تُسهل عليه معرفة الكلام المباشر (Direct Speech) والكلام غير المباشر (Indirect Speech).

(3) وفيما يلي المفردات التي تستعمل في الصيغتين المذكورتين أعلاه: المفردات في حالة الكلام المباشر. وهي تعبيرات تخص الزمان والمكان ... وتتغير متى تغيرت الجملة إلى الكلام غير المباشر الأمر الذي لا بد من إجراء التغيرات اللازمة في صيغ الأفعال وكذلك الضمائر.

الكلام المباشر Direct Speech	الكلام غير المباشر Indirect Speech
Today – tomorrow	That day – the next day
Last night	The night before
Now	Then
Yesterday	The day before

205

This – these	That – those
Here – there	There
Next week	The following week
Ago	Before
Present simple tense	Past simple tense
Present continuous tense	Past continuous tense
Present perfect tense	Past perfect tense
Past simple tense	Past perfect tense
Future simple tense	Future past tense
Thus	So
Said to	Told
say	Tell

(4) لاحظ التغييرات التالية سواء كانت في الكلام المباشر(Direct Speech) أم في الكلام غير المباشر (Indirect

Speech) ويأتي الكلام المباشر بين أقواس دائماً مثل الجملة الاخبارية التالية:

The waiter said, «I cannot return today».

قال الخادم: « لا أستطيع أن أعود اليوم» (كلام مباشر).

ولكن في حالة نقل الكلام المباشر إلى الكلام غير المباشر تُحذف الأقواس وتضاف كلمة (that) أمام (said)

ويتغير الضمير من (I) إلى (he) ويتغير الفعل المضارع إلى فعل ماضي وكذلك ظرف الزمان . مثل:

أما إذا بدأ المتكلم أو استعمل الفعل   The waiter said that he could not return that day.

المضارع (say) أو (says) حينئذ تبقى الجملة على ما هي

دون تغيير في الزمان إلا الضمير. والكلمات المدونة في الجدول تخضع للتغير مثل:

Statement:

The waiter says, "I cannot return today".

a-

The waiter says that he cannot return today.

The students say, "the lesson is not difficult".

b-

They say that the lesson is not difficult.

إذن لاحظت كيف تم التغيير في جملتي (a) وفي جملتي (b) في زمن المضارع. ولا بد أنك لاحظت كذلك الفاصلة أمام فعل (said) و(say) وهي ضرورية في الكلام المباشر.

Direct Speech and Indirect Speech

لاحظ أنه عندما تُجرى عملية التغيير من الكلام المباشر إلى غير المباشر أو بالعكس لا بد من مراعاة نوعية الكلام المكون من الآتي:

Kinds of sentences	أنواع الجمل
1- statement	1- جملة اخبارية
2- question	2- سؤال
3- order, command – request	3- أمر / طلب
4- exclamation	4- تعجب

١- تستعمل كلمة (if) أو (whether) عند التغيير للسؤال الحالي من أدوات الاستفهام (what – who – when
– how - where -) من الكلام المباشر إلى الكلام غير المباشر مثل:

Questions:

1 - "Have you got a garden?".

   - He asked if (whether) I had got a garden.

2 - Ali said to the teacher, "Is the lesson difficult"?

   - Ali asked the teacher whether the lesson was difficult?

3 - "Does the man water the garden?".

   - "Shall I have a holiday tomorrow?"

   - He asked whether he would have a holiday the next day.

لاحظ أن هناك كلمات عند استعمالها في الكلام المباشر تتغير مع الكلام الغير المباشر مع مراعاة تغير
الأفعال من المضارع إلى الماضي.

Direct Speech		Indirect Speech	
said	قال	asked	سأل
Said to	قال إلى	asked	سأل
Says to	يقول إلى	Asks	يسأل

Direct Speech	Indirect speech
(1) Layla said to Lamya: "Where is my blue dress?"	Layla asked Lamya where her blue dress was.
(2) Ali says to his friend Mustafa: "Which book can I read tomorrow?".	Ali asks his friend Mustafa which book he can read the next day.
(3) I said to the waiter: "what time is it now?"	I asked the waiter what time it was then.
(4) "Shall I open the book?"	He asked whether (if) he should open the book.
(5) "Shall I do it before tomorrow"	He asked if he should do it the next day.

لاحظ استعمال الكلمات التالية مع صيغة الأمر (command) وفيما يلي جدول الكلمات التي تستعمل

عندما يتغير الكلام المباشر من صيغة الأمر المباشر إلى الكلام الغير المباشر.

Direct Speech	Indirect Speech	
Said	ordered	أمر
Said	Commanded	صدر أمراً
Said	Requested	طلب

Said	Prayed	توسل/ تضرع
Said	Begged	التمس/ استجدى
Said	Told	قال
Said	advised	نصح/ حذر/ أوصى

لاحظ أن كل كلمة من الكلمات المذكورة آنفاً تختلف اختلافاً واضحاً عند استعمالها في التغير مـن الكلام المباشر إلى الكلام غير المباشر. كما يجب وضع كلمة (to) قبل الفعل مثال:

Direct Speech	Indirect speech
1- He said: "Open the door".	He ordered me to open the door.
2- He said: " Go to sleep".	He told me to go to sleep.
3- "Come to the lesson", said the teacher.	The teacher requested me to come to the lesson.
4- My father said to the servant: "Bring me the food here in my office".	My father ordered the servant to bring him the food there in his office.

ونأتي الآن إلى صيغة التعجب التي لها العديد من الكلمات الخاصة بالكلام المباشر وهي للتعبير عـن الفـرح أو الاستحسان والاستغراب أو الحزن أو الاشمئزاز إلخ والمستعملة فقط في المحادثة ولكن عند تغير الكـلام المباشر إلى الكلام الغير المباشر تُستعمل بعض الكلـمات كبـديل لهـا مـع مراعاة جميـع التغيـيرات في زمـن الأفعال والضمائر وإدراج (that).

Direct Speech	Indirect speech
1- Alas!	Said with regret.
2- How beautiful	Said with satisfaction.
3- How nice!	Said with pleasure.
4- How bad!	Said with sorrow.
5- How ugly!	Said with regret
6- My goodness!	Said with sadness.
7- What a dirty place!	Said with anger
8- What a fool!	Said with distress
9- Oh!	Said with sadness
10- Help me!	Shouted to
11- Oh dear!	Said with remorse
12- There	Shouted to
13- Hail!	Greeted with respect
14- Too bad!	Said with sadness
15- Long live!	Shouted with joy
16- Hurrah!	Shouted with satisfaction
17- What a great mistake!	Cried with sorrow.
18- How sorry!	Said with sorrow.

The meaning of these words | معاني الكلمات التالية

Exclamation | تعجب

Alas! | واحسرتاه!

How beautiful! | ما أجمله/ ما أجملها!

211

How nice!	ما ألطفه/ ما ألطفها!
How ugly!	ما أقبحه/ ما أقبحها!
Hello! Hallo!!	للترحيب أو للتعجب (أو للإجابة على الهاتف
My goodness!	يا إله!
What a dirty place!	ما أقذره هذا المكان!
Oh!	أوه! (صوت يعبر به عن الدهشة أو الألم)
Help me!	ساعدني! النجدة!
What a fool!	كم هو سخيف/ ما أسخفه!
Oh dear!	يا إله!
There!	هناك!
Hail!	للترحيب/ للتحية!
Too bad!	سيء جداً!
Long live!	يحيا/ يعيش!
Hurrah!	تستعمل للهتاف!
What a mistake!	يا له من خطأ!
Ugh! (oof)	للتعبير عن الاشمئزاز أو القرف من شيء. (أُف)

Regret	أسف/ ندم	Sadness	حزن
Satisfaction	رضاء	Distress	محنة/ قلق
Pleasure	سرور	Remorse	ندامة
Sorrow	حزن/ أسى	Joy	سعادة/ فرح

Dir. (1) The shopkeeper said: "Alas! I have lost my money".

Ind.   The shopkeeper said with regret that he had lost his money.

Dir. (2) The tourist said, "How beautiful this place is".

             The tourist said with satisfaction that the place was beautiful.

Dir. (3) The teacher said, "How nice this student is".

Ind.   The teacher said with pleasure that the student was nice.

Dir. (4) Ali said: "How ugly this man is".

Ind.   Ali said with sorrow that that man was ugly.

Dir. (5) The director of the museums said: "Hello" to all the tourists who came to visit one of the museums of the country.

Ind.   The director of the museums greeted all the tourists who had come to visit one of the museums of the country.

Change the following into indirect speech.

لاحظ: قبل حل التمرين راجع دائماً القواعد.

Direct Speech:

1- The student said: «This lesson is not easy at all today».

2- The teacher says: «You must do the exercise today».

3- I said to my father: «I always read my lessons well. I want to pass the examination».

4- Layla says to her mother: «I do not like to go to swim today».

5- «We can read and write English well», said the boys in this school.

6- «You told me a new story today», said the student to his father

7- My father said to me: «Take your bag with you to school everyday».

8- The servant said: «I do not know how to cook fish at all».

9- The farmer has said to his children: «You are all lazy boys. You must work hard in this farm if you want to be well-off».

Indirect Speech:

1- ....

2- ....

3- ....

4- ....

5- ....

6- ....

7- ....

8- ....

9- ....

Exercise (30):   تمرين (30):

Change the following into indirect speech.

1- I said to my friend: "Is your school far away?

2- The boy said to his father: "Are there one thousand dirhams in a dinar?"

3- "Don't you go to school on Friday?" said the man.

4- "Do you stay at home in winter?. Don't you go out?" said his friend Ali.

5- "Did your father arrive in Morocco yesterday?" said the boy.

6- "Hasn't he been here since Monday?".

7- "Are knives made of metals?".

8- "Can you tell me why you left the class?".

9- "Is it true that this lesson is easy?".

10- "Was your mother glad of you success?".

11- "Have you any more of this fruit?".

12- "Have you the new tickets of the train?"

13- "Has she got any flowers in the garden?".

14- "Did you have a new lesson today?".

15- "Is there anytime for another cup of tea?".

16- My friend said: "Who went with you to Paris?"

17- Ali said to Ahmed: "Which of these lessons is the best?".

18- The student said: "Where is my place in this class?".

19- The foreigner said to the driver: "Which bus goes to Tripoli?".

20- The man said: "What is wrong with the clock?".

21- The policeman said to Ali: "What is your friend's name and why is he without the driving license?"

22- The tourist said to the policeman: "Which is the nearest way for us to the station?".

23- The teacher said to the pupil: " What is the matter with you today? Haven't you done your homework?".

24- The inspector said to Mustafa: "Which of these students here is your brother?".

25- The shopkeeper said to the woman here: Which dress is this, mine or yours?".

Indirect Speech

1- ....

2- ....

3- ....

4- ....

5- ....

6- ....

7- ....

8- ....

9- ....

10- ....

11- ....

13- ....

14- ....

15- ....

16- ....

17- ....

18- ....

19- ....

20- ....

21- ....

22- ....

23- ....

24- ....

25- ....

Exercise (31):   **:(31) تمرين**

Change the following into indirect speech.

1- He said to me:«Please go away from this place».

2- She said to the student: «Come soon, please».

3- The teacher said to the servant: «Close the school».

4- His father said to the teacher: «Please , my son will be absent today».

5- The teacher said to all students in the class: «Read slowly so you can understand your lessons well».

6- The director said to the employee: «Bring here all the files of the hotel».

7- Ali said to his friend Ahmed: «Come with me to watch the football match with my family today».

8-The student's father said to the teacher: «My son does not Know how to spell my proper name».

9- His neighbour said to his friend: «Never take the new car without my permission».

10- «Do not drive my car at night». Said the father to his son.

Indirect Speech

1- ....

2- ....

3- ....

4- ....

5- ....

6- ....

7- ....

8- ....

9- ....

10- ....

Exercise (32): تمرين (32):

Change the following into indirect speech.

1- The shopkeeper said: "Alas! I have lost my money today".

2- The tourist said: "How beautiful this place of pictures is!".

3- The teacher said: "How nice this student is!".

4- Ali said: "How ugly this man is!"

5- The director of the museum said: "Hello!" to all the new tourists who came to visit this museum today.

6- Ali's mother said: "My goodness! You cut yourself with this bad knife".

7- The policeman said to the owner of this hotel: "What a dirty place this is".

8- "Oh" I said. "I forgot to bring the lesson with me today".

9- "Help me!" he said to the policeman.

10- What a fool you are! said the owner of the car to the driver today.

11- The man here said: "Oh dear! I have lost my bag of money on my way to the station today".

12-The foreigner said to the officer: "There! The thief is standing near the red car".

13- The host said: "Hail!" to all the guests when they arrived to his new house.

14- The trainer of the blue football team said: "Too bad!" when he heard the news of the defeat of his team today.

15-The soldiers said: "Long live the general!".

16- The Arabs everywhere shouted: "Hurrah! We won the war against our enemy in 1973s".

17- The cook cried: "What a mistake I made today! I forgot to prepare the food for the new guests today".

18- The students said: "Ugh! the teacher did not explain this important lesson to us today!".

New words:	الكلمات الجديدة:
The foreigner	الأجنبي
The host	المضيف
The guests	الضيوف
The trainer	المدرب
Museums	المتاحف
The director	المدير
The football team	فريق كرة القدم
Defeat	هزيمة
Won فعل ماضي	ظفر/ فاز/ انتصر

Indirect Speech

1- ....

2- ....

3- ....

4- ....

5- ....

6- ....

7- ....

8- ....

9- ....

10- ....

11- ....

13- ....

14- ....

15- ....

16- ....

17- ....

18- ....

تعبيرات شائعةLesson Thirty Nine

الدرس التاسع والثلاثون

Common Expressions

Common Expressions	**تعبيرات شائعة:**
Ok – (Okey)	حسناً مظبوط/ أنا موافق
Excuse me	المعذرة/ اسمح لي/ العفو
How much does this cost?	كم ثمن هذا؟
It is very dear.	غالٍ جداً
It is very cheap.	رخيص جداً
Permit me to do this.	اسمح لي أن أقوم/ أن أفعل هذا
Believe as I do.	أعتقد كما أعتقد
It is good news.	خبر طيب/ أخبار طيبة
I have no knowledge of the matter.	لا علم لي بالموضوع
Do you want to know the case	هل تريد أن تعلم بالقضية
Poverty is not a shame it is rather a shame to be lazy	ليس الفقر عيباً ولكن العيب أن تكون كسولاً
That is to say.	يعني/ أعني
Neither my father nor my mother knew about this bad case.	لا أبي ولا أمي عرفا بالقضية الرديئة

Do not be pessimistic	لا تكن متشائماً
I have nothing to do with the matter at all.	لا علاقة لي بالأمر / بالمسألة إطلاقاً
Neither this nor that is good	لا هذا ولا ذاك ينفع
How are you?	كيف حالك؟
Do as we do everyday	اعمل مثلما نعمل كل يوم
I shall wait here until he comes	سأنتظر هنا حتى يأتي
Had it not been for my father, that man would have been in prison because he is innocent.	لولا والدي لكان ذلك الرجل في السجن لأنه بريء
Were it not for that man, my car would have been stolen.	لولا ذلك الرجل لكانت سيارتي سرقت
Had I known of the case before, I would have refused it.	لو عرفت بالقضية من قبل لرفضتها
If my brother comes to you tell him that I am ill.	إذا جاء أخي إليك قل له إني مريض.
If you should go there, I would go with you.	إذا ذهبت هناك أذهب معك.
He who sows reaps	من يزرع يحصد
How lovely the sky is!	ما أجمل السماء!
How difficult this man is!	ما أصعب هذا الرجل
How loathsome is injustice!	ما أقبح الظلم
How red this apple is!	ما أشد احمرار هذه التفاحة!

How kind they are!	ما أكرمهم! ما ألطفهم!
It was a good day's journey.	إنها كانت رحلة ليوم كامل
He is truly good man	إنه رجل صالح/ رجل نافع
Our work is in the interest of the whole	عملنـا/ خـدمتنا في سبيل المـصلحة العامـة/ الفائدة العامة
This time	هذه المرة
This man is as good as his word.	هذا الرجل/ هذا الانسان صادق الوعد
In my case this is my case.	بأية حال/ مهما يحدث هذه هي قضيتي
He bought the farm in the name of his brother.	اشترى المزرعة باسم أخيه
This is the right solution	هذا هو الحل الصحيح/ الملائم
He is the right man for this department.	هـذا رجـل مناسـب/ ملائـم لأجـل هـذه المصلحة/ الإدارة
I saw the man, he is all right again.	رأيت الرجل هو في صحة جيدة مرة ثانية
He is the right owner of this shop.	هو صاحب/ مالك الحانوت الشرعي
This man is a straight thinker.	هذا رجل حصيف التفكير
He gave me a straight report..	أعطاني تقريراً صريحاً موثوقاً
This car is in use.	هذه السيارة رهن الاستعمال

This car is out of use.	هذه السيارة ليست معدة للاستعمال
They received him with a warm welcome.	استقبلوه بترحيب حماسي
I always try to read the papers between the lines.	أحاول دائماً أن أقرأ الجرائد بين السطور
Let's go! Let us go! Come on!	هلّم بنا!
How often?	كم مرة؟

This passage reads differently

تقرأ هذه الفقرة على نحو مختلف

He said to the man: "It is a point of no return".	قال للرجل: "إنها نقطة اللارجوع".
Be happy!	افرح!
Write!	أكتب!
Tell!	اخبر!
Get up!	قم!
Cast!	ارم!
Stretch out!	تمدّد!
Bring!	إحضر!
Never mind!	لا بأس!
Come!/ Come on!	تعال! هَلُمَّ!
Fine/ Superb!	ممتاز!

Good – bye	بأمان الله/ في أمان الله
This is reasonable	هذا معقول
Of course/ Certainly	طبعاً بالتأكيد
Would you be kind as to tell me where is a good restaurant here.	مـن فضلك/ هـل لـك أن تخـبرني/ تـدلني عـلى مطعم جيد هنا
And so forth/ and so on	هلم جراً وهكذا دواليك
So long so	طالما/ شرط أن
Bring me! Give me! Get me!	هَلُمَّ/ هات!

Conversation:

Vocabulary	مفردات الحديث
Let us talk/ write	دعنا نتحدث/ نكتب/ إلخ
To my opinion	في اعتقادي/ حسب رأيي
Please do	تفضل/ افعل
Ready	جاهز
Interested	مهم
May/ might	يمكن/ مَكَّنَ
Therefore	لذلك
Main	رئيسي
Such as	مثل
Will do abroad	ينفع في الخارج
I don't think so	لا أعتقد/ لا أظن ذلك

Social Science	العلم الاجتماعي
Archeology	علم الآثار
Biology	علم الأحياء
Surgery	الجراحة
Phonetics	علم الأصوات اللغوية
Finance	علم المالية
Administration	علم الإدارة
Physics	علم الفيزياء
Psychology	علم النفس
Geometry	علم الهندسة
Any how – in any case however	على كل حال
And so forth/ and so on	وهلم جراً
Salient	هام/ مهم
Nowadays	في هذه الأيام
In addition to	بالإضافة إلى
Notable subjects	مواضيع جديرة
Worthy of notice	جدير بالملاحظة
Lack of	عدم/ لا وجود
Understanding	تفاهم/ فهم
Prevent	عائق/ حاجز/ معرقل رئيسي
Prevent	يمنع/ يحول دون/ يعوق

Approach	يتقارب/ يقرب من/ يتقارب إلى
Cast and thought	اهتمام/ نظام وتقاليد
Few of	قليل من
Knowledge	معرفة/ علم
Together	معاً/ مع بعض
Lead	يقود/ يرشد/ يدل
Cordial	ودي/ ودية
Customs	عادات
Relations	علاقات/ صلات/ روابط
Cordiality	مودة/ قلبياً/ مودة
Cordially	مودة/ قلبياً
Contact	يتصل/ اتصال/ يتعرف/ احتكاك
Really	حقيقة/ حقاً
probably	ربما/ تقريباً

Conversation between Ali and Ahmed:

Ali	:	Let us begin! Ahmed.
Ahmed	:	Yes, what do you want to know from me?
Ali	:	I like to ask you a few questions.
Ahmed	:	Please do; I am ready to answer any question you like.
Ali	:	Are you really interested to study English?
Ahmed	:	Yes, I am very much interested to study it.

Ali	:	Why are you so much interested to study it?
Ahmed	:	Because I may some day wish to travel abroad. It will then be of some use to me, for it is not really good to ask somebody to be your translator for everything. Therefore, to my opinion, it is necessary that one should at least know a foreign language. However, it is not necessary to be this language, but any other European language; such as Italian or French will probably do abroad.
Ali	:	Do you really think, Ahmed, that a study of a foreign language, nowadays, is only for the use of traveling abroad?
Ahmed	:	No, I do not certainly think so. It is not only used of traveling abroad but it is used for many other things. However, to study a foreign language is very much useful to know other people's history, customs, economics and political systems. Language is, in any case, a salient medium for anyone wishing to translate anything of interest or to further one's own studies in different subjects such as Social Science, Archeology, Biology, Phonetics, Finance, Economics, Surgery, Psychology, Geometry and so forth.
Ali	:	What do you have to say on this subject?
Ahmed	:	I wish to tell you that I read in our great history that when the Arabs had been united as one great nation, a lot of people of different races had tried to learn their language in order to know their religion, science and their great civilization.
Ali	:	Yes, that is true and because the Arabs were a very strong nation.

Ali	:	In addition to these notable few subjects, there is another subject worth of notice; that is to say, the lack of understanding each other's language is considered, by a lot of people, the main barrier that prevents an approach between people of different cast and thought.
Ahmed	:	Yes, I believe you are quite right. Therefore, we agree that the knowledge of a language undoubtedly leads to cordial relations amongst peoples who may come into contact with others.

Religion	الدين
Races	أجناس/ شعوب
Culture	حضارة
Let	يدع/ يجيز/ يسمح/ يترك
Let the man have a home	دع الرجل يملك منزلاً
They let the visitor go home	سمحوا للنزيل بالذهاب إلى بيته
Let	يؤجر/ يستأجر
Ali lets rooms to students	يؤجر علي الغرف للطلبة
This room lets for five dinars a day.	إيجار هذه الغرفة خمسة دنانير في اليوم
Let's go fishing	دعنا نذهب لصيد السمك
Let everyman do his duty	دع كل واحد يعمل واجبه
Let in	يدخل

Let know	يعلم
Let go	يطلق سراحه
Civilization	المدنية

Exercise (33): تمرين (33):

Answer the following questions:

1- What does Ali want to know from Ahmed?

2- What is the main subject of the conversation?

3- Why is Ahmed so interested to study English?

4- Is it true that a foreign language is only useful for traveling abroad?

5- For what a foreign language is useful other than traveling abroad?

6- What do you think that prevents people to approach each other in the past and in the present?

Exercise (34): تمرين (34):

Make questions for these answers:

1- I am interested to study English.

2- I wish to go abroad when I finish my studies in my country

3- It is not good, in my opinion to ask somebody to translate things for you.

4- It is really useful and interesting to know other people's language.

5- Because the whole Arab people had been a great united nation.

6- A knowledge of a language certainly leads to cordial relations.

Vocabulary to be memorized:	مفردات للحفظ:
Country	ريف – وطن – بلد
Town	مدينة
Specially	خاصة
Remember	تذكر/ يتذكر
Remember me to him	أهدي إليه تحياتي
Healthier than	أكثر صحة من
Europe	أوروبا
Rare (reir)	نادر
Out of	خارج عن
Medical treatment	معالجة طبية
Fresh air	جو منعش/ جو نقي
He was fresh and gray	كان مفعماً بالنشاط
His memory is still fresh	ذاكرته لا زالت طرية
Fresh news	أخبار جديدة
Side	جانب
Remain	يمكث
As a matter of fact	في واقع الأمر
Else	آخر/ أيضاً/وإلا
How else	بطريقة أخرى
What else shall I do?	ماذا سأعمل أيضاً؟

Run, else you will be late	إجري وإلا ستكون متأخراً
Elsewhere	في مكان آخر
Somebody else	شخص آخر
What else do you want?	ماذا تريد آخر؟
Height	ارتفاع/ علو
Width	عرض/ اتساع
Centimeter	سنتمتر
Inch/ inches	بوصة/ بوصات
Yard/ s	ياردة/ ياردات
Meter	متر
Weight	وزن/ ثقل
Foot/ feet	قدم/ أقدام
Program	منهج
Newspaper	صحيفة/ جريدة
Map	خريطة
Note-book	دفتر
Means of transportation	وسائل النقل
House – a storehouse	منزل/ مخزن
Home – homeless people	مسكن/ أناس من غير سكن
Colleague	زميل/ رفيق
Associate	شريك/ عضو

Companion	رفيق/ زميل
Fellow	رفيق/ قرين/ وليف
Fellow – citizen	مواطن
fellowship	رفقة/ صحبة/ زمالة

Vocabulary to be memorized (1):	**مفردات للحفظ:**
1- master	سيد/ مدرس/ أستاذ/ رب عمل
2- masters	أسياد/ مدرسون/ أساتذة/ أرباب عمل
3- Mister	سيد/ وتكتب (.Mr) عادة
4- Messrs	أسياد/ وتكتب (.Messrs)
5- Madam	سيدة
6- gentle	نبيل/ كريم
7- gentleman	رجل كريم/ سيد
8- business	عمل/ مشروع/ تجارة
9- antiquity – antiquities	آثار
10- judgment/s	حكم/ أحكام
11- customer/s	زبون/ زبائن
12- potatoes	بطاطس
13- pigeon/s	حمامة/ حمام
14- sweets	حلويات
15- beans	لوبيا/ فول

16- sugar	سكر
17- salt	ملح
18- tomatoes	طماطم
19- tea	شاي
20- vegetables	خضار
21- cucumber	خيار
22- dates	تمر
23- eggs	بيض
24- fish	سمك
25- fowl	لحم دجاج
26- figs	تين
27- fruit salad	فاكهة متنوعة
28- grapes	عنب
29- garlic	ثوم
30- green beans	لوبيا خضراء
31- jam	مربى
32- lamb	خروف
33- meat	لحم
34- melon	بطيخ أصفر / شمام
35- water melon	بطيخ أحمر
36- mutton	لحم ضان

37- oranges	برتقال
38- oil	زيت
39- olive	زيتون
40- onion	بصل

Vocabulary to be memorized (2):	**مفردات للحفظ:**
apricots	مشمش
Beef	لحم بقر
Butter	زبدة
Broad beans	فول/ باقلي
Cabbage	ملفوف/ كرنب
Chestnut	الكستناء
Cauliflower	قرنبيط
Chicken	فروج/ لحم دجاج
Cakes	كعك
Cheese	جبنة
Coffee	قهوة
Chocolate	شوكولاته
Cream	القشطة
Vinegar	خل
Soup	حساء/ شوربة

Vocabulary to be memorized (3):	**مفردات للحفظ:**
Birds	طيور
Dog	كلب
Wolf	ذئب
Hyena	ضبع
Lion	أسد
Tiger	نمر
Lioness	لبوة
Gorilla	غوريلا
Peacock	طاووس
Goose	إوزة
Hen	دجاجة
Wolf	ثعلب
Rabbit	أرنب
Donkey	حمار
Stork	اللقلق
Panda	دب/ البندة
Ape	قرد
Hoopoe	الهدهد
Hare	الأرنب الوحشي
Game	الصيد

Vocabulary to be memorized (4):	مفردات للحفظ:
Parts of the body	أجزاء جسم الإنسان
Ankle	رسغ القدم
Arm	ذراع
Back	ظهر
Cheek	خد
Chin	ذقن
Chest	صدر
Colon	القولون
Ears	آذان
Elbows	المرفقان
Eyebrows	الحواجب
Eyes	عيون
Face	وجه
Foot – feet	رجل/ أرجل
Finger	اصبع
Forehead	جبهة
Gall bladder	المرارة
Hand	يد
Head	رأس
Hair	شعر

Heart	قلب
Heel	عقب القدم
Jaw	فك
Knee	ركبة
Knuckles	مفاصل الأصابع
Left lung	الرئة اليسار
Right lung	الرئة اليمين
Legs	السيقان
Lips	شفاه
Liver	كبد
Mouth	فم
Nose	أنف
Neck	رقبة
nostril	المنخار

Lesson Forty

الدرس الأربعون

استعمال اسم الفاعل كصفة

The use of past participle as an adjective

يستعمل اسم الفاعل (أي التصريف الثالث) وهو الــ... (Past Participle) كصفة أمـام الإسـم ويتكيّـف مـع الاسم سواء كان في المفرد أو الجمع.

Example:

مثل:

1- The closed window.	النافذة المقفولة.
2- The closed windows.	النوافذ المقفولة.
3- All the doors are open (صفة).	جميع الأبواب مفتوحة.
4- The open windows.	النوافذ المفتوحة.
5- I see there an open box.	أرى هناك (صندوقاً مفتوحاً).
6- an open country.	بلد مفتوح.
7- open air.	العراء/الهواء الطلق
8- open air.	حرية الدخول/ الباب المفتوح
9- open-eyed.	مفتوح العينين/يقظ
10- openhanded.	كريم/سخي/مبسوط اليد

ونجد كذلك أن الفعل المنتهي بحرف (ing) مثل: (writing) يُستعمل كصفة أي يصف الإسم ويسمى (Present Pariciple).

1- a smoking room	حجرة التدخين
2- a sweeping victory	انتصار كاسح
3- a smiling face	وجه مبتسم
4- a sleeping coach	حافلة النوم
5- a sleeping car	عربة النوم
6- a dining room	حجرة الأكل
7- an inviting offer	عرض جذاب/ مُغرٍ

Exercise (35):

a- Give these verbs their present participle:

تمرين (35):

اجعل لهذه الأفعال اسم الفاعل في حالة المضارع:

1- To swim	1- ....
2- To get	2- ....
3- To come	3- ....
4- To want	4- ....
5- To hear	5- ....
6- To know	6- ....
7- To wish	7- ....
8- To drive	8- ....
9- To do	9- ....
10- To sell	10- ....

b- Give these verbs their past participle:

اجعل لهذه الأفعال اسم الفاعل في حالة الماضي:

1- To tell	1- ………………………………
2- To run	2- ………………………………
3- To carry	3- ………………………………
4- To teach	4- ………………………………
5- To eat	5- ………………………………
6- To speak	6- ………………………………
7- To try	7- ………………………………
8- To ride	8- ………………………………
9- To fight	9- ………………………………
10- To live	10- ………………………………

Exercise (36):

تمرين (36):

How to express in English the following sentences:

كيف تعبّر بالإنجليزية عن الجمل التالية:

1- كم ثمن هذا البيت؟

1- ………………………………………………………

2- اسمح لي أن أقوم بهذا العمل الجديد.

2- ………………………………………………………

3- لا علم لي بهذا الموضوع إطلاقاً.

3- ………………………………………………………

4- هل تريد أن تعلم (أن تكون على علم) بهذه القضية؟

4- ………………………………………………………

241

5- ليس الفقر عيباً.

5- ....

6- ولكن العيب أن يكون المرء كسولاً.

6- ....

7- لا علاقة لي بالموضوع بتاتاً.

7- ....

8- لا أريد هذا البيت ولا ذاك الحقل.

8- ....

9- اعمل دائماً الخير للآخرين. ستكون سعيداً.

9- ....

10- سوف أنتظر حتى يأتي الرجل هنا.

10- ....

Exercise (37):   تمرين (37):

Complete in English the Arabic phrases or sentences:

أكمل بالإنجليزية المفردات أو الجمل العربية المكتوبة أدناه:

1- Ali will ride.....................   دراجته الجديدة غداً

2- He will go.....................   إلى المدرسة بدراجته غداً

3- Layla will be.....................   غائبة غداً لأنها مشغولة جداً

4- The teacher has.....................   كتب الدرس على اللوح

5- The doctor has.....................   لم ير المريض الجديد

6- The sister has.....................   رأت المريض، جالساً على سريره

7- We shall not.....................   ننسى أن نقرأ دروسنا غداً

8- Will they come.................	إلى المتحف اليوم؟
9- I want to go.....................	معك إلى بيت صديقنا
10- This book is...................	لك
11- Ali's family....................	ذهبت إلى باريس يوم أمس
12- They will go.....................	بدونه لأنه لديه دروس كثيرة
13- I do not need	هو
14- I am not in need...............	له
15- I shall be in.....................	معك في الحديقة
16- I live in Beirut and.............	وبيتي قرب هذا الشارع
17- He is going.....................	ليقرأ دروسه في حجرته
18- She is going....................	لتدرس قصتها بعد غد
19- I am going.....................	لأراه الليلة في المنزل
20- We are going..................	لكي نكتب رسالة إلى صديقنا علي
21- Are you going.................	لتقود الدراجة الجديدة اليوم؟

Conversation: محادثة:

Ali:	See those two teachers, Ahmed.
Ahmed:	Yes, I see them. They are sitting after they had given the lessons to their students. I am sure, they are talking about the type of the English exams for the next summer.
Ali:	Yes, I heard something about that story of exams. But it is a long time ago.

Ahmed:	Do you think, Ali, that those two teachers will set out a difficult examination for the secondary school at the end of the year?
Ali:	No, I don't think so. Generally my dear Ahmed, the exams, as far as I understand, are prepared in accordance with both the book and the previous lessons. They can never be based upon new information or studies.
Ahmed:	Yes, you are right in this case.
Ali:	Thank you. There is one more thing to bear in mind, Ahmed. I always wanted to say it.
Ahmed:	Yes, what is it, Ali?
Ali:	In my opinion, no one can ever succeed if he has not been careful about his studies all the year.
Ahmed:	That is correct. Success in school comes from intelligence and careful studies.

Vocabulary	مفردات
sure	متأكد/ثابت/واثق
type	نوع/شكل
next summer	الصيف المقبل
long time ago	منذ عهد بعيد/من مدة طويلة
set out	يشرع/يجهز/يبدي/يعرض
prepare	يُعد/يجهز/يهيئ/يصوغ
for sure	من غير ريب/ بدون شك

I don't think so!	لا أظن ذلك
generally	عادة/عموماً
in accordance with	طبقاً لـ.../وفق/بناء على
as far as I understand	إلى حد ما أفهم
both	كلاهما
previous	سابق
information	معلومات
to bear in mind	يضع نصب عينيه/يتذكر
never mind	لا بأس/لا تقلق
correct	صحيح/مضبوط
success	نجاح
careful	حذر/يقظ/شديد الحرص
intelligence test	اختبار الذكاء
intelligence	ذكاء/فكر
standard	مستوى/قياسي
according to	طبقاً لـ....

Exercise (38):

تمرين (38):

a- Answer the following questions:

Q- 1- What are the two teachers doing? Where?

A-   ……………………………………………………

Q- 2- Why are they sitting?

A-   ……………………………………………………

Q- 3- To whom had they given their lessons?

A-   ....

Q- 4- About what do you think the teachers are talking?

A-   ....

Q- 5- What will be the standard of the examinations?

A-   ....

b- Make questions for the following answers.

A- 1- The conversations is about the examination.

Q-   ....…......?

A- 2- The examinations will be for the next summer.

Q-   ....…......?

A- 3- I think the examination will not be difficult.

Q-   ....…......?

A- 4- Examinations are prepared according to the book.

Q-   ....…......?

A- 5- Success comes from intelligence and careful studies all the year.

Q-   ....…......?

Lesson Forty One　　　　　　　　　　الدرس الواحد والأربعون

تقوية المخزون اللغوي ببعض المفردات والجمل المفيدة

Enriching Knowledge with some Vocabulary and sentences

Banking Affair Vocabulary:

المعاملات المصرفية. المفردات الخاصة بالمصارف.

affair	مسألة/شأن/شؤون تجارية
account/s	حساب/حسابات
article/s	مادة/مواد
bank/s	مصرف/مصارف
branch/es	فرع/فروع
business	عمل/أعمال
cheque book	دفتر صكوك
cost	ثمن/نفقة/كلفة
current price	السعر الحالي/الجاري
current rate	السعر/القيمة التجارية
coins	عملة/عملات معدنية
cash	نقداً/أوراق نقدية
currency	عملة متداولة

company	شركة
draft	سحب
dinar/s	دينار
exchange	مقايضة/تبادل
export	يصدر السلع
import	يستورد السلع
establish	يثبت/يقدم
firm	شركة
firm/company	مؤسسة/شركة
foreign	خارجي
general	عام
house	بيت تجاري
lend	يعير/يقرض
lawyer/s	محامي/محامون
loan/s	قرض/قروض بفائدة/بفوائد
merchant/s	تاجر/تجار
money	نقود/عملة
notary	الموثق العام
note	مذكرة
notebook	مفكرة
note of hand	كمبيالة/صك تعهدي

notice	إشعار/إعلان/إنذار
at short time	من غير مهلة كافية
to take notice	يرى/يلاحظ/ينتبه
business address	عنوان تجاري
open an account	فتح حساب
bankruptcy	إفلاس
payment	تسديد
price	ثَمن/سعر
purchase	شراء
product	إنتاج/محصول
rate	سعر الخصم
securities	كفالة
sell/sold	يبيع/باع
store	مخزن
settle	يسدد
tax/es	ضريبة/ضرائب
transactions	إجراء/إجراءات/معاملات/صفقات
sell for cash	يبيع نقداً
on credit	يبيع بالدَّين
a power of attorney	الوكيل/المحامي
settlement	تسديد مدفوعات

a letter of exchange	رسالة مقايضة
a letter of credit	رسالة اعتماد
thank you very much	شكراً كثيراً
for the payments	على جميع المدفوعات

Useful phrases	**جمل مفيدة**
Would you be kind	هل تتكرم/من فضلك
to direct me to a bank here?	ترشدني إلى مصرف هنا؟
Certainly/of course.	طبعاً/بالتأكيد/من غير شك
Where must I change	أين يجب/ينبغي علي استبدال
my money, please?	نقودي، من فضلك؟
in this bank here	في هذا المصرف هنا
I don't know	لا أعرف
How much is the exchange	كم هو سعر الاستبدال
today, please?	اليوم/ من فضلك؟
I am sorry, I don't know	آسف/إني آسف لا أعرف
how much is the exchange	كم هي قيمة الاستبدال
rate in this bank today	في هذا المصرف اليوم
I want to exchange	أريد أن أستبدل
100 (one hundred dollars)	مئة دولار
100 (one hundred sterling)	مئة استرليني

100 (one hundred dinars)	مئة دينار
Please verify the rate	من فضلك تأكد من السعر
for me	لأجلي
I found that the prices are	وجدت أن الأسعار
very high here in this country	مرتفعة جداً في هذه البلاد/ في هذا البلد
No, it is not true	لا، هذا غير صحيح/هذا ليس صحيحاً.
The prices are very low	الأسعار منخفضة جداً
Since I know the rates	حيث/ بما أني أعرف الأسعار
I shall now go to the	سوف أذهب الآن إلى
nearest exchange office.	أقرب مكتب استبدال عملة
Yesterday, I went to the	أمس ذهبت إلى
Bank of Commerce	المصرف التجاري
In this bank I opened	في هذا المصرف فتحت
a current account	حساباً جارياً
I left some money	تركت بعض النقود
as a deposit in the bank	كرصيد في المصرف
After that the bank gave me	بعد ذلك أعطاني
a cheque book	المصرف دفتر صكوك
How the payments are to be	كيف تكون المدفوعات
made, in cash or cheques?	نقداً أم بالصكوك؟
Both payments are valid	كلتا المدفوعات

in this bank	صحيحتان/مقبولة
Will you please, now that	من فضلك، بعد أن سددت
I settled my account	حسابي
forward all the articles	أرسل جميع المواد
to my address in Lebanon	إلى عنواني في لبنان

Conversation	محادثة:
Introduction phrases	عبارات التعارف:
May I introduce myself	اسمح لي أن أقدم نفسي
My name is Ahmed	اسمي أحمد
This is Ali and that is Qasem	هذا علي وذاك قاسم
Make your selves comfortable	تفضلوا استريحوا
Help yourself	تفضل (اخدم نفسك بنفسك)
Help yourselves	تفضلوا (اخدموا نفسكم بنفسكم)
To your health	في صحتك
Would you like	هل تحب/هل ترغب
to drink tea?	تشرب شاي؟
to drink coffee?	تشرب قهوة؟
to drink lemonade?	تشرب عصير ليمون؟
Do you smoke?	هل تدخن؟
No, I don't smoke at all	لا، لا أدخن إطلاقاً

No, we don't smoke at all	لا، لا ندخن إطلاقاً
I don't want to drink	لا أريد أن أشرب
any thing for the time being	أي شيء في الوقت الحاضر
Thank you very much	شكراً كثيراً
for your kind invitation	على دعوتكم الكريمة
Good luck	حظ سعيد
Good - bye	مع السلامة
Call a doctor	أطلب طبيب/دكتور
at the doctor's clinic	عند عيادة الطبيب
doctor	طبيب
clinic	عيادة
hospital	مستشفى
treatment	معالجة/علاج
Please call a doctor here	من فضلك أريد طبيباً هنا
I fell ill today	أشعر بأني مريض اليوم
I have pain in my...	عندي ألم/ صداع في
head	رأسي
stomach	معدتي
mouth	فمي
tongue	لساني
it is dry	إنه جاف

I felt sick yesterday	شعرت بالتقيؤ يوم أمس
I felt some dizziness	شعرت بدوار وبدوخة
I have flu/influenza	عندي أنفلُونزا
because of cold	نتيجة/بسبب البرد
Please doctor I have	من فضلك/يا دكتور
indigestion	عسر هضم
I have lost appetite	لقد فقدت الشهية
I have toothache	عندي ألم/عندي وجع سن
I am not diabetic	لست مصاب
(diabetes)	بداء البول السكري
Please, give me your	من فضلك أعطني
prescription	الوصفة
How much	كم
I owe you?	عليّ أن أدفع؟
Thank you very much	شكراً جزيلاً
I shall try to send	سأحاول أن أرسل/أبعث
someone for the medicine today	أحد للأدوية اليوم
I am sorry, I am late today	آسف إني متأخر اليوم
It is high time to go	آن الأوان لكي نذهب
now – at present	الآن – حالياً – في الوقت الحاضر
now that…	الآن وقد.....

Lesson Forty Two　　　　　　　　　　　　الدرس الثاني والأربعون

استعمال النقط في اللغة

The use of punctuations

لاحظ لماذا تُستعمل النقط المختلفة كالفاصلة (،) (Comma) والفواصل المعكوسة المزدوجة مثل («....»)

وتسمى (Inverted commas) والفاصلة المنقّطة (;) وتسمى (semicolon) وعلامة الترقيم وهي عبارة عـن

نقطتين (:) وتسمّى (colon) وعلامة الوقف الكامل (.) وتسمى (The full stop) وعلامة الاسـتفهام أو أداة

الاستفهام (؟) (Question Mark) وعلامة التعجب (!) وتسمّى (Exclamatory Mark) ثم بعد هذه العلامـات

وعددها عشرة نأتي إلى ما يسمى بالحرف الاستهلالي أي الحرف الكبير الذي تم شرحـه في بدايـة الكتـاب في

الدرس الأوّل. والحروف الكبيرة تسمى في اللغـة الإنجليزيـة (Capital Letters) والحـروف الـصغيرة (Small

Letters) إذن الجواب للسؤال الذي بدأنا به الدرس هو: أولاً يستطيع الدارس الـذي اسـتوعب اسـتعمالاتها

جيداً أن يفهم ما يقرأه عن الغير، وثانياً يستطيع أن يُفْهِم الآخرون ما كتبه. والآن نبدأ من جديد:

1- تستعمل الفاصلة (،) (comma) مباشرة بعد الجملة وتعني التوقف قليلاً مثل: There are, indeed, very

She kept cats, :في مثل (and) وكما تستعمل الفاصلة لعدم تكرار حـرف العطـف.few pupils in the class

:مثل ،However وتوضع الفاصلة بعد كلمة .. dogs, rabbits, and parrots at home

However, I saw him yesterday.

We were late for dinner, nevertheless, we found it.

2- توضع الفواصل المعكوسة («.....») وتسمى (Inverted commas) بين جملة أو فقرة مقتبسة على سبيل الاستشهاد والاقتباس هو (Quotation marks) وتستعمل أيضاً للكلام المباشر (Direct Speech) مثل: Ali's

teacher said: «Everyone must write his name».

3- تستعمل الشولة المنقوطة (;) (Semicolon) بعد كل جملة لتعني التوقف أكثر من الفاصلة مثل: In the Ali's library we can buy books of history, arithmetic, journalism and philosophy; in the other library, in the same street, we can only buy books for children.

4- تستعمل علامة الترقيم أو الشارحة عندما نقف قليلاً لنقارن بين تعبيرين أو بين بيانين وهي عبارة عـن نقطتين (:)(Colon).

It was early winter: All the country was really full of snow.

5- تستعمل علامة الوقف الكامل (.) (Full Stop) للإشـارة إلى القـارئ أن الجملة انتهـت وليس هنـاك مـا يـضاف إليهـا مثل: Some people like to swim in winter. But Others do not like to swim except in summer. The book is new, I bought it today. It is a good one. It costs very little. It is not expensive.

حاول أن تمعن النظر فـ في الجمل لترى أن لكل جملة Full Stop.

6- توضع أداة الاستفهام مباشرة بعد الاستفهام مثل: Who told you that? Where are you going? How do you know my name? How do you do? (The Interrogation mark) إذن بعد الجملة.

7- توضع أداة التعجب عند نهاية الجملة مثل:

What a beautiful car!

Come here!

Don't go away!

Don't write this word anymore!

(The exclamation mark) إذن عرفت كيف ومتى تستعمل

8- تُستعمل الحروف الكبيرة (Capital Letters) لعدة أغراض منها:

(1) عند بداية الجملة الجديدة Lebanon is in Asia.

(2) عند بداية الفواصل المعكوسة. He said: «Go away».

(3) تُستعمل للأسماء. Ali, Mustafa, Layla, Lamya.

(4) تستعمل للعواصم والمدن والجبال المشهورة: Beirut, Syria, Albarok, Laytani.

(5) يتكوّن الضمير أنا (I) من حرف كبير وكذلك الألقاب مثل: آنسة (Miss) سيدة (Mrs). سيد (Mr.).

الدرس الثالث والأربعون

جمل مفيدة

Useful Phrases

- It matters very little.	- لا يهم كثيراً.
- We don't know whether	- لا نعرف أن
to go or not.	نذهب أم لا.
- He is always happy	- هو دائماً سعيد
whether sick or well.	سواء أكان مريضاً أم معافى.
- I got my money by	- تحصّلت على نقودي
a narrow margin.	بشق النفس.
- This is not a laughing	- هذا شيء أو موضوع جدي
matter, my dear friend.	إلى حد بعيد يا صديقي.
- This is a serious matter.	- هذا موضوع جدي أو خطير.
- As a matter of fact	- في الواقع/ في حقيقة الأمر.
- flatters	- يتملّق
- He flatters so that	- يتملّق لكي/لعلّه
he may win a fovour.	يمكن أن يفوز بخدمة/عطف.
- As far as I know they	- بقدر ما أعرف/ أعلم
have not yet come to the office.	لم يأتوا بعد إلى الآن إلى المكتب.

- They have not yet come	- لم يأتوا بعد إلى المكتب
as far as I know to the office.	بقدر/بحسب ما أعلم.
- How is your business?	- كيف حال مشروعك/مشاريعك؟
- So far so good is	- مشروعي/مشاريعي على ما يرام حتى الآن.
my business.	
- from head to foot	- من قمة الرأس إلى أخمص القدم.
- from head to toe.	- من الرأس إلى أصبع القدم.
- Carry your book as a	- احمل كتابك
close friend wherever you go.	كصديق قريب حيثما تذهب.
- It was a narrow escape.	- كانت نجاة بشق النفس.
- His marks were of a	- علاماته ضئيلة/
narrow majority.	بأكثرية ضئيلة.
- He is a narrow minded man.	- إنه رجل ضيّق التفكير.
- The owner of this car	- صاحب هذه السيارة
was worse off.	كان أشد فقراً/أشد سوءاً.
- The owner of this car	- صاحب هذه السيارة
was better off.	كان في أحسن حال.
This man plays with	- يلعب هذا الرجل
with his left hand.	بيده اليسرى.
- You must go to the left	- يجب أن تذهب إلى اليسار
first, turn to the right.	أولاً، ثم اتجه إلى اليمين.

- You will find my school.	- سوف تجد مدرستي.
- I was there last year	- كُنت هناك السنة الماضية
with my schoolmates.	مع رفقاء مدرستي.
- I don't want to be	- لا أريد أن أكون
the last in my school.	الأخير في مدرستي.
The lesson, as for me, is easy.	الدرس، بالنسبة لي سهل/هين.

Conversation (a)	**محادثة**
post office	مكتب بريد
airmail	بريد جوّي
seamail	بريد بحري
stamp/s	طابع/طوابع بريدية
registered letter/s	رسالة مسجّلة/رسائل مسجّلة
telegram/s/cable/s	برقية/برقيات
envelope/s	ظرف رسالة/ظروف
signature	توقيع
address/es	عنوان/عناوين
telephone	هاتف
fee/s	رسم/رسوم بريدية
P.O.B. (Post Office Box)	اختصار (صندوق بريد)
amount	قيمة

261

urgent	مستعجل
letter box	صندوق بريد
telegram-form	قسيمة/نموذج للبرقيات
postman	ساعي بريد
postcard	بطاقة بريدية
receiver	المستلم
sender	المرسل
delivery	تسليم
parcel	طرد/رزمة

(B) Conversation:

Ahmed:	Please, Ali
	Where is the post office in this town?
Ali:	Why do you want to know the post officc?
Ahmed:	Because I have a letter which I want to send to my father by airmail.
Ali:	Where is your father now?
Ahmed:	My father is now in Paris.
Ali:	What does he do in Paris?
Ahmed:	He studies Economy there.
Ali:	That is a very important subject today.
Ahmed:	Oh! yes, it is true but he has not sent any news about him for a long time.
Ali:	Then, take my advice, try to send him a telegram which is quicker than an airmail letter.
	He will receive it earlier than the letter.

Ahmed:	I think I will take your advice, so let's go the post office to take the telegram-form and write a few words to my father whom I need very badly these days.
Ali:	Yes, let's go together to finish your desire, my dear Ahmed.
Ahmed:	I must thank you for your advice.
Ali:	Don't mention it. It is my duty to help my friends.
Ahmed:	It was a wonderful opinion which was better than sending a letter by airmail.

Exercise (39):   تمرين (39):

Answer the following question:

(1) What does Ahmed want from Ali?

....

(2) How does Ahmed want to send his letter?

....

(3) To whom does Ahmed want to send the letter?

....

(4) Why does Ahmed want to send his letter?

....

(5) Where is his father?

....

(6) Why is Ahmed's father in Paris?

....

(7) Which is quicker to Ahmed a letter or a telegram?

....

الأعداد

Numbers

Cardinal Numbers: الأعداد الأصلية:

1	One	واحد
2	Two	اثنان
3	Three	ثلاثة
4	Four	أربعة
5	Five	خمسة
6	Six	ستة
7	Seven	سبعة
8	Eight	ثمانية
9	Nine	تسعة
10	Ten	عشرة
11	Eleven	أحد عشر
12	Twelve	اثنتا عشر
13	Thirteen	ثلاثة عشر
14	Fourteen	أربعة عشر

15	Fifteen	خمسة عشر
16	Sixteen	ستة عشر
17	Seventeen	سبعة عشر
18	Eighteen	ثمانية عشر
19	Nineteen	تسعة عشر
20	Twenty	عشرون
21	Twenty-one	واحد وعشرون
22	Twenty-two	إثنان وعشرون
23	Twenty-three	ثلاث وعشرون
24	Twenty-four	أربع وعشرون
25	Twenty-five	خمسة وعشرون
26	Twenty-six	ست وعشرون
27	Twenty-seven	سبع وعشرون
28	Twenty-eight	ثمانية وعشرون
29	Twenty-nine	تسع وعشرون
30	Thirty	ثلاثون
31	Thirty-one	واحد وثلاثون
32	Thirty-two	اثنان وثلاثون
33	Thirty-three	ثلاثة وثلاثون
34	Thirty-four	أربع وثلاثون
35	Thirty-five	خمس وثلاثون

36	Thirty-six	ست وثلاثون
37	Thirty-seven	سبع وثلاثون
38	Thirty-eight	ثمان وثلاثون
39	Thirty-nine	تسع وثلاثون
40	Forty	أربعون
50	Fifty	خمسون
60	Sixty	ستون
70	Seventy	سبعون
80	Eighty	ثمانون
90	Ninety	تسعون
100	One hundred	مئة
101	One hundred and one	مئة وواحد
200	Two hundred	مئتان
300	Three hundred	ثلاثة مئة
400	Four hundred	أربع مئة
500	Five hundred	خمس مئة
1000	One thousand	ألف
2000	Two thousand	ألفان
3000	Three thousand	ثلاثة آلاف
4000	Four thousand	أربعة آلاف
5000	Five thousand	خمسة آلاف

1000.000	One million	مليون
2000.000	Two million	مليونان
3000.000	Three million	ثلاثة ملايين

ملاحظة: إن الأرقام الإنجليزية تأتي قبل الاسم باعتبارها صفة، مثل:

Example:

Give me one book. There are one hundred books in my library. I saw thousands of students in the university today.

Ordinal number: **العدد الترتيبي:**

كتابة	مختصر		
first	1st	الأولى	الأول
second	2nd	الثانية	الثاني
third	3rd	الثالثة	الثالث
fourth	4th	الرابعة	الرابع
fifth	5th	الخامسة	الخامس
sixth	6th	السادسة	السادس
seventh	7th	السابعة	السابع
eighth	8th	الثامنة	الثامن
ninth	9th	التاسعة	التاسع
tenth	10th	العاشرة	العاشر

Fractional Number: **العدد الكسري:**

كتابة	مختصر		
a half	$\dfrac{1}{2}$		النصف
a quarter	$\dfrac{1}{4}$		الربع
three-quarters	$\dfrac{3}{4}$		ثلاثة أرباع

269

two thirds	$\dfrac{2}{3}$		الثلثان
one-fifth	$\dfrac{1}{5}$		الخمس
one-sixth	$\dfrac{1}{6}$		السدس
two fifths	$\dfrac{2}{5}$		خمسان
one-seventh	$\dfrac{1}{7}$		السبع
three-fifths	$\dfrac{3}{5}$		ثلاثة أخماس
one-eighth	$\dfrac{1}{8}$		الثمن
two-eighths	$\dfrac{2}{8}$		ثمنان

الدرس الخامس والأربعون

مفردات الوقت والطقس

Time and Weather phrases

The days of the week	أيام الأسبوع
Sunday	يوم الأحد
Monday	يوم الاثنين
Tuesday	يوم الثلاثاء
Wednesday	يوم الأربعاء
Thursday	يوم الخميس
Friday	يوم الجمعة
Saturday	يوم السبت
weekday	يوم الأسبوع
weekend	نهاية الأسبوع
weekly	أسبوعياً
daily	يومياً
the date	التاريخ
time	الوقت
Don't be late	لا تتأخر
come in time	تعال في الموعد

at dawn	في الفجر
at dusk	في الغسق
before day	قبل بزوغ الفجر
day and night; night and day	ليلاً نهاراً/طول الوقت
one of these days	عما قريب/في المستقبل القريب
some day	في يوم ما/في المستقبل
the other day	منذ بضعة أيام

The months of the year	شهور السنة الميلادية
1- January	يناير/ كانون الثاني
2- February	فبراير/ شباط
3- March	مارس/ آذار
4- April	أبريل/ نيسان
5- May	مايو/ أيار
6- June	يونيو/ حزيران
7- July	يوليو/ تموز
8- August	أغسطس/ آب
9- September	سبتمبر/ أيلول
10- October	أكتوبر/ تشرين الأول
11- November	نوفمبر/ تشرين الثاني
12- December	ديسمبر/ كانون الأول

1- northward			نحو الشمال
2- southward			نحو الجنوب
3- eastward			نحو الشرق
4- westward			نحو الغرب
5- date			تاريخ
6- What is the date today?			ما هو التاريخ اليوم؟

The four seasons: **الفصول الأربعة:**

1- Spring   1- الربيع

2- Summer   2- الصيف

3- Autumn   3- الخريف

4- Winter   4- الشتاء

The Cardinal Points: الجهات الأصلية:

1- North	شمال	northern	شمالي
2- South	جنوب	southern	جنوبي
3- East	شرق	eastern	شرقي
4- West	غرب	western	غربي

Vocabulary (time)   **مفردات (الوقت الزمن)**

sunrise   شروق الشمس

273

time	وقت – زمن
hour	ساعة زمنية
minute	دقيقة
second	ثانية
sunset	غروب الشمس
tide	المد والجزر
wait	ينتظر
a day	يوم بكامله
dawn	فجر
morning	صباح
noon	الظهر
midday	نصف النهار
afternoon	بعد الظهر
evening	مساء/غروب
night	ليل/ هبوط الليل
midnight	نصف الليل
month	شهر
year	سنة
week	أسبوع
daylight	ضوء النهار

Telling the time	الساعة كم؟
- I like to see the	أحب أن أرى/ أن أشاهد
natural colors	الألوان الطبيعية
of both the sunrise	لكل من الشروق
and the sunset in	والغروب في
my country.	بلادي.
- The days are longer in summer	الأيام في الصيف أطول
than in winter.	من الأيام في الشتاء
- The light of a lamp is not	ضوء المصباح ليس
so good for the eyes as	هكذا جيداً للنظر مثل
the daylight.	ضوء النهار
- Man lived in caves before	عاش الإنسان في الكهوف
the dawn of history.	قبل فجر التاريخ.
- caves	كهوف
- man/men	الإنسان
- the dawn of history	فجر التاريخ
- era	عصر/دهر
- horizon	أفق
- A new era of understanding	بزوغ عصر جديد
is dawning in the horizon.	للتفاهم في الأفق.
- Ali spends his time in the	علي يقضي وقته في

English		Arabic
evening watching		المساء يشاهد
the television.		الإذاعة المرئية (التلفاز).
- Tell him that I shall be		أخبره/ قل له بأني سأكون
there in a minute.		هناك في لحظة/ في دقيقة.
- He gave me		أعطاني/ قدم لي
minute instructions.		تعليمات دقيقة
about how I must do		حول كيفية ما يجب علي
my work in the office.		أن أعمل في المكتب
- The minute you see him,		في اللحظة/ في الدقيقة التي تراه
coming, please, tell me.		آتٍ، أرجو أن تخبرني.
- 60 minutes make		ستون دقيقة
an hour.		تساوي ساعة
- 24 hours make a day.		أربع وعشرون ساعة تساوي يوماً.
- My clock strikes		ساعتي تعلن
the hours and the half		الساعات وأنصاف الساعات
hours in the room.		في الحجرة.
- My breakfast hour is		ساعة فطوري (هي)
always at eight every		دائماً الثامنة كل يوم
day except Friday.		ما عدا يوم الجمعة.

What is the time please?   **كم الساعة من فضلك؟**

It is 1 o'clock.	one	الساعة – 1

It is 2 o'clock.	two	الساعة – 2
It is 3 o'clock	three	الساعة – 3
It is 4 o'clock	four	الساعة – 4
It is 5 o'clock	five	الساعة – 5
It is 6 o'clock	six	الساعة – 6
It is 7 o'clock	seven	الساعة – 7
It is 8 o'clock	eight	الساعة – 8
It is 9 o'clock	nine	الساعة – 9
It is 10 o'clock	ten	الساعة – 10
It is 11 o'clock	eleven	الساعة – 11
It is 12 o'clock	twelve	الساعة - 12

It is 12 $\frac{1}{2}$ (Twelve and half) (12-30)

الساعة $12\frac{1}{2}$

It is 12,45 (It is quarter to one) ($12\frac{3}{4}$)

الساعة 12,45

It is 5 minutes past one

الساعة الواحدة وخمس دقائق.

It is half past eleven

الساعة $11\frac{1}{2}$

لاحظ: تستعمل كملة (past) بمعنى (و) عندما تكون مثلاً:

It is five (past) one

الساعة الواحدة (و) خمس دقائق

وتستعمل كلمة (to) بمعنى (إلا) عندما تكون مثلاً:

It is 5 (to) one	الساعة الواحدة إلا خمس دقائق
What time is it now?	كم الساعة الآن؟
It's one o'clock now	الساعة الواحدة الآن
It's midday	نصف النهار
It's midnight	نصف الليل
It's ten minutes (to) ten	الساعة العاشرة إلّا عشر دقائق
	في المحادثة يُستغنى عن كلمة (it is) ويقال مثلاً:
five minutes past twelve	الساعة 5-12
ten minutes past twelve	الساعة 10-12
15 minutes past twelve	الساعة 15-12
a quarter (past) twelve	الساعة 15-12
half (past) twelve	الساعة 30-12
thirty-five minutes (past) one	الساعة 35-1
twenty-minutes (to) one	الساعة 40-12
a quarter (to) one	الساعة 45-12
five minutes (to) one	الساعة 55-12
One o'clock	الساعة 13:00 (الساعة الواحدة)

What time is it now? It is one o'clock.

Vocabulary	مفردات
a wrist watch	ساعة يد
a wall clock	ساعة حائط

an alarm clock	ساعة منبهة
my watch is slow	ساعتي متأخرة
my watch is fast	ساعتي متقدمة
my watch stopped	ساعتي توقفت
it does not work	ساعتي لا تعمل
I want to take my watch	أريد أن آخذ ساعتي
to the watchmaker for	إلى الساعاتي
repairing it today	لتصليحها اليوم
early	مبكراً/باكراً
punctual	دقيق/في المواعيد
late	متأخراً
to set	يضبط/يرتب/يثبت

The weather	**الطقس**
Vocabulary	**مفردات**
1- cold	بارد
2- hot	حار/حام
3- rain	مطر
4- temperature	درجة الحرارة
5- mild	معتدل/لطيف
6- degree/s	درجة/درجات
7- gradually	تدريجياً
8- thermometer	ميزان الحرارة
9- climate	المناخ
10- variable	متغير/متقلب
11- influence	تأثير
12- desert	صحراء
13- region/s	إقليم أقاليم
14- tolerable	مقبول/ممكن احتماله
15- air	هواء/نسيم
16- wind	غبار/رماد
17- dust	غبار/رماد
18- storm/s	عاصفة/عواصف

19- frost	متجمّد/تجمُّد/مُثلج
20- heat	حرارة/طقس حار
21- cloud	سحاب
22- snow	ثلج
23- north wind	ريح شمالي
24- west wind	ريح غربي
25- south wind	ريح جنوبي
26- east wind	ريح شرقي
27- mountain/s	جبل/جبال
28- Mediterranean	البحر الأبيض المتوسط
29- air condition	مكيّف
30- barometer	مقياس الضغط الجوي
31- snow storm	عاصفة ثلجية
32- lightning	البرق
33- hurricane	إعصار
34- thunder	هدير/ترعد
35- sunshine	مشمس/أشعة الشمس/إشراق
36- warm	دافئ/حار
37- hot weather	طقس حار/حام
38- cold weather	طقس بارد

Conversation about the weather

- Since you are near the window

you can tell me how is the

weather today.

- What is the weather

like today?

- Yes, I can tell you.

- It seems that the weather is

fine today.

- It is neither cold

nor hot in this place.

- I think, there will be

rain later on.

- Look at the thermometer

and see how many

degrees we have today.

- My thermometer in my

room indicates

15 degrees as far as

I know up to now.

- بما أنك قريب من النافذة

تستطيع أن تخبرني

عن الطقس اليوم.

- ما نوع الطقس

اليوم؟

- أجل أستطيع أن أخبرك.

- يظهر أن الطقس

ممتاز/منعش/ رائع اليوم.

- إنَّه لا بارد

ولا هو حار في هذا المكان.

- أعتقد سيكون

هناك مطر في ما بعد.

- أنظر إلى مقياس الحرارة

وأبصر كم هي الدرجات

أو كم عندنا من الدرجات.

- مقياس الحرارة في حجرتي

يشير إلى 15 درجة

بقد ما أعرف/ أو

بقدر ما أعلم حتى الآن.

- Generally speaking	عادة/ على العموم
the climate in the Middle East in	الشرق الأوسط
January is very cold.	شهر يناير/كانون ثاني برد شديد.
- In other parts of	في أجزاء أخرى من
the Middle East	الشرق الأوسط
January is the coldest.	شهر كانون الثاني هو الأبرد في السنة.
- While August is the	بينما شهر آب
hottest in the year in	هو الأحر في السنة
North Africa.	شمال أفريقيا.
- The temperature in winter	درجة الحرارة في الشتاء
along the coast is	على طول الساحل
usually tolerable.	عادة ممكن احتمالها.
- However, some countries	- على كل حال، بعض
in the Middle East have	الأقطار في الشرق الأوسط
variable climate	لديها (مناخ) متقلب وذلك
because of the influence	بسبب تأثير
both the sea and	البحر
the desert.	والصحراء معاً.
- On the contrary	بالعكس/ على العكس تماماً
we have a mild winter	لدينا/ عندنا شتاء معتدل
in Lebanon.	غير حاد/ بارد في لبنان.

- We have to leave before

the storm.

- The yearly rainfall in

England is heavy.

علينا أن نترك قبل

قبل مجيء العاصفة.

هطول المطر السنوي في

انجلترا قوي/شديد.

Lesson Forty Six

الدرس السادس والأربعون

الأفعال الشاذة

Irregular verbs

Present Tense	Past Tense	Past Participle	الترجمة في المضارع
1- go	went	gone	يذهب
2- grow	grew	grown	يزرع/ينمو/ينبت
3- have	had	had	يملك/عنده
4- hear	heard	heard	يسمع/يصغي
5- hide	hid	hidden	يختبئ/يخفي
6- hit	hit	hit	يضرب/يخبط
7- hold	held	held	يمسك/يقبض على
8- hurt	hurt	hurt	يُؤذي/يضر
9- keep	kept	kept	يحتفظ/يصون
10- kneel	knelt	knelt	يركع/يبرك
11- know	knew	known	يعرف/يعلم/يدري
12- lay	laid	laid	يضع/يحط/يبسط
13- lead	led	led	يقود/يرشد/يتقدم
14- lean	leant (ed)	leant (ed)	يسند/يَتَّكئ/يميل
15- leap	lept (ed)	lept (ed)	يقفز/ينط

285

Present Tense	Past Tense	Past Participle	الترجمة في المضارع
16- learn	learnt (ed)	learnt (ed)	يتعلم/يدرس/يعرف
17- leave	left	left	يترك/يأذن
18- lend	lent	lent	يسلف/يعطي
19- let	let	let	يطلق/يطلق سبيله
20- lie	lay	lain	يتمدد/يرقد/يستلقي
21- light	lit (lighted)	lit (lighted)	يشعل/يلقي ضوءاً على
22- lose	lost	lost	يفقد/يضيع/يخسر
23- make	made	made	يعمل/يصنع/يُشَكِّل
24- mean	meant	meant	يقصد/يعني
25- meet	met	met	يلتقي بـ/يتقابل
26- mislead	misled	misled	يضل/يخدع
27- misspell	mispelt (ed)	mispelt (ed)	يخطئ في التهجئة
28- mistake	mistook	mistaken	يخطئ/يغلط
29-misunderstand	misunderstood	misunderstood	يسيء التفهم/أو الفهم
30- overcome	overcame	overcome	يتغلب على/ يقهر
31- pay	paid	paid	يدفع/يؤدي/يفي
32- put	put	put	يضع/يحط/يعرض
33- read	read	read	يقرأ/يطالع
34- rid	rid	rid	يخلِّص/يحرر

286

Present Tense	Past Tense	Past Participle	الترجمة في المضارع
35- ring	rang	rung	يدق/يقرع
36- rise	rose	risen	يقيم/ينهض/يرتفع
37- run	ran	run	يجري/يركض/يدير
38- saw	sawed	sawed	ينشر الخشب/يقطع
39- say	said	said	يقول
40- see	saw	seen	يرى/يشاهد/يتصور
41- seek	sought	sought	يقصد/يبحث
42- sell	sold	sold	يبيع/يتجر
43- send	sent	sent	يرسل/يبعث
44- set	set	set	يضع/يركّز
45- shrink	shrank	shrunk	ينكمش
46- shake	shook	shaken	يهز/يزعزع
47- shine	shone (ned)	shone (ned)	يلمع/يشرق
48- show	showed	showed	يظهر/يعرض
49- shut	shut	shut	يقفل/يغلق
50- sing	sang	sung	يغني/يغرد
51- sit	sat	sat	يجلس/يقعد
52- sleep	slept	slept	ينام/يرقد
53- smell	smelt (lled)	smelt (lled)	يشمّ

Present Tense	Past Tense	Past Participle	الترجمة في المضارع
54- speak	spoke	spoken	يتكلم/ينطق
55- spend	spent	spent	يصرف/ينفق
56- spread	spread	spread	ينشر
57- stand	stood	stood	يقف
58- steal	stole	stolen	يسرق
59- strike	stroke	struck	يضرب
60- sweep	swept	swept	يكنس
61- take	took	taken	يأخذ
62- teach	taught	taught	يعلم
63- think	thought	thought	يفكر
64- throw	threw	thrown	يرمي
65- understand	understood	understood	يفهم/يدرك
66- undertake	undertook	undertaken	يأخذ على نفسه
67- write	wrote	written	يكتب/يسجل

اختبارات ذاتية مع مفتاح أجوبة التمارين

اختبار رقم واحد

Test No. One

من تمرين رقم (1)

إلى تمرين رقم (8)

From Exercise (1)

to Exercise (8)

Letters (a-b-c-d-e-f-g-h) حروف

Test No. one

اختبار رقم واحد

لاحظ أن هذا الاختبار مستمد من الدروس السابقة.

(a) Put (a) or (an) or (the)

where required. Ex. 1:

(أ) ضع أداة النكرة أو التعريف

في المكان المطلوب في هذا التمرين 1:

1- He is .... man.

2- Put .... books on the table.

3- .... officer has .... bicycle.

4- Cows give us .... milk.

5- He is .... farmer.

6- Make for me .... appointment.

(b) Put the following nouns

In their proper columns Ex. 2:

(ب) ضع الأسماء التالية في العمود

الخاص بها. تمرين 2:

goodness	Cairo	Sanine	Damascas
crew	Ahmed	Suez canal	Amira
sugar	car	table	Everest
The Nile	cat	dog	difficulty
Proper	**Nouns of**	**Nouns Of**	**Nouns of**
Nouns	**Animals**	**Capitals**	**Mountains**
(1)	(1)	(1)	(1) ....
(2)	(2)	(2)	(2) ....

291

Nouns of Rivers & Canals	Names of things	Abstract Nouns	Collective Nouns
(1)	(1)	(1)	(1) ....
(2)	(2)	(2)	(2) ....

(c) Put the following countable or uncountable

nouns in the

blank spaces:

(ج) ضع الأسماء التالية القابلة

للعد والتي لا تقبل للعد

في المكان الشاغر:

(1) milk (2) trousers (3) water (4) car (5) bell (6) butter (7) class (8) cheese (9) egg (10) ice.

Countable Nouns

1- ....

2- ....

3- ....

4- ....

5- ....

Uncountable Nouns

1- ....

2- ....

3- ....

4- ....

5- ....

(d) Translate the following

words into English

(د) ترجم الكلمات التالية

إلى الإنجليزية.

1- ....

2- ....

3- ....

السعداء

الضعفاء

الصغار

4- ……………………………..	الشجعان
5- ……………………………..	الأغنياء
6- ……………………………..	هذا رجل مُسن
7- ……………………………..	ذلك رجل سعيد
8- ……………………………..	هذه امرأة فقيرة
9- ……………………………..	لبناني

(e) put the following possessive

Adjectives in the bank spaces:

(هـ) ضع صفات الملكية
التالية في المكان الشاغر:

My – his – her – its – our – your – their.

1- I have a farm; it is ………. farm.

2- You have a newspaper; it is ……….. newspaper.

3- He has a magazine; it is ……. magazine.

4- She has a house; it is ……….. house.

5- It has a ball; it is ……… ball.

6- We have a car; it is …….. car.

7- They have some eggs; they are ………… eggs.

(f) Make the following plural:

(و) اجعل الآتي في حالة الجمع:

1- My farm is in my land.

2- He has his lesson in his house.

3- She has her doctor in her school.

4- The dog has its food in its hut.

5- The cat has its ball in its hut.

6- My mother is in the house of my friend.

7- His sister is now in the classroom.

8- There is an Englishman in the farm.

9- This is its food.

10- That is her house in the big garden.

(g) change the names into

pronouns:

(ز) حول الأسماء إلى ضمائر مناسبة

في الأماكن الشاغرة:

1- Ali has a radio; it is ……….. radio.

2- Amira has a paper; it is …….. paper.

3- Layla and Naima have a ball; it is ……….. ball.

4- Ali and Yousef are in ……….. classroom.

5- Father and mother are in ……… house.

(h) Put the possessive pronoun

in the blank space:

ضع ضمير الملكية في

المكان الشاغر:

1- This is my radio; it is ………..

2- That is his utensil; it is …………..

3- Those are our apples; they are ………

4- These are their books; they are ……..

5- My pen is here; it is …………..

6- Are these your shoes? Yes, they are………

7- Is this money yours? No, it is not ……….

8- My friend has my apples; they are …………..

9- His friend has his bicycle; it is …………..

10- She has a cat in the house; It is …………

11- They have some cars; they are ………..

12- It has a ball; it is ………………

اختبار رقم اثنان

Test No. Two

من تمرين رقم (1)

إلى تمرين رقم (12)

From Exercise (1)

to Exercise (12)

Test No. Two

(a) correct the verbs in brackets

1- The dog (to go) to the garden everyday.

2- We (to write) our letters every two weeks.

3- The boy (to carry) his bag every morning.

4- Ali often (to know) his lesson well.

5- Amira (to try) to learn English well.

(b) Use these verbs in sentences:

(1) To want (2) To know (3) To sell (4) To speak (5) To write (6) To ride (7) To tell (8) To eat.

(c) Make these sentences negative:

1- She gets her newspaper everyday.

2- They write their lessons in their houses.

3- He studies everyday.

4- We go to sleep early.

5- You sit at home alone.

(d) Make these sentences interrogative:

1- I go to school everyday except Sunday.

2- My father works in his field.

3- Ali comes home early.

4- He finished his lesson last night.

5- We waited for him here in the station yesterday.

اختبار رقم إثنان

(1) صحّح هذه الأفعال بين قوسين:

(2) استعمل هذه الأفعال في جمل:

(3) اجعل هذه الجمل في حالة نفي:

(4) اجعل هذه الجمل في حالة الاستفهام:

(e) Make these sentences

in the present simple tense:

1- I went home to sleep last night.

2- He came to school very late yesterday.

3- She went to the hairdresser last week.

4- He told his story to the officer this evening.

5- The train ran to Saida last month.

(f) Show which is the subject

and the object in these sentences and put them

in the proper column:

1- They generally swim in this pool.

2- He always wants some food for his dog.

3- Ali often knows his lessons well.

4- Amira sometimes wishes to go to France.

5- The teacher teaches English in this room.

(5) اجعل هذه الجمل في زمن المضارع البسيط:

(6) بين أيهما المبتدأ والخبر في هذه الجمل
وضعهما في الأعمدة الخاصة بها:

الخبر/ المفعول به (Object Predicate)	المبتدأ/الفاعل Subject
1- …………………………	1- …………………………
2- …………………………	2- …………………………
3- …………………………	3- …………………………
4- …………………………	4- …………………………
5- …………………………	5- …………………………

(g) Make these verbs into useful sentences

(Present Simple Tense):

(7) اجعل هذه الأفعال في جمل مفيدة في حالة

المضارع البسيط:

1- To believe in.   6- To contain.

2- To care for.   7- To desire.

3- To consist of.   8- To hear.

4- To hate.   9- To wish.

5- To know.   10- To study.

1- I believe in God.   نموذج:

2- ....

3- ....

4- ....

5- ....

6- ....

7- ....

8- ....

9- ....

10- ....

(h) Then make the same ten sentences in (g) in

into Past Simple Tense:

(8) ثم اجعل نفس هذه الجمل العـشرة في حـرف

(g) في زمن الماضي البسيط:

1- I believe in God.   نموذج:

2- ....

3- ....

4- ....

5- ……………………………………

6- ……………………………………

7- ……………………………………

8- ……………………………………

9- ……………………………………

10- ……………………………………

(i) Correct the verbs in brackets in the Present Simple Tense or in the Present Continuous Tense:

(9) اكتب الأفعال التالية في زمن المضارع المستمر:

1- He always (to go) to school) early.

2- I (to finish) my work now.

3- She (to learn) Arabic every morning.

4- They (to go out) at the present time.

5- We (to tell) the story last week.

6- Ali (to play) music now.

7- Layla (to study) English now.

8- Lamya (to go) to her friend yesterday.

9- He (to come) to work very soon.

(j) Write down the following verbs in the Continuous Tense:

(10) أكتب الأفعال التالية في زمن المضارع المستمر:

to go – to write – to do – to learn – to tell.

1- ……………………………………

2- ……………………………………

3- ……………………………………

4- ……………………………………

5- ……………………………………

(k) write down the above sentences in the past

Continuous Tense:

(11) ثم اكتب الجمل المذكورة أعلاه في زمن الماضي

المستمر:

1- ....

2- ....

3- ....

4- ....

5- ....

(l) Use the verbs in brackets as verbal nouns

(gerund) (ing):

(12) استعمل الأفعال بين قوسين في حالة أو صيغة

المصدر:

1- To smoke	....	6- To play	....
2- To study	....	7- To write	....
3- To read	....	8- To give	....
4- To swim	....	9- To eat	....
5- To speak	....	10- To have	....

اختبار رقم ثلاثة

Test No. Three

من تمرين رقم (1)

إلى تمرين رقم (11)

From Exercise (1)

to Exercise (11)

Test Number Three

Exercise (1)

(a) Put the following sentences into Future
Continuous Tense:

1- I shall name the man ....

2- We shall lead our car. ....

3- He will decide the trip. ....

4- She will visit the new farm. ....

5- You will admire his work. ....

6- He will assure her wishes. ....

7- I shall want a telephone. ....

8- We shall go to the station. ....

9- They will appreciate his work. ....

10- The train will arrive. ....

(b) Translate the following words into English:

1- ....

2- ....

3- ....

4- ....

5- ....

6- ....

اختبار رقم (3)

تمرين رقم (1)

(أ) ضع الجمل الآتية في صيغة
المستقبل المستمر:

(ب) ترجم الكلمات التالية إلى اللغة الإنجليزية:

1- لم يذهب إلى مكتبه اليوم.

2- لا يتكلمون الإنجليزية جيداً.

3- لم أراه اليوم.

4- لم يجد النقود على المنضدة أمس

5- لا نريده أن يذهب إلى فرنسا اليوم.

6- لا تستطيع أن تشتري هذه السيارة.

7- ....

8- ....

9- ....

10- ....

11- ....

7- الطقس حار في الصيف وبارد في الشتاء.

8- هو رجل كريم لأنّه غني جداً.

9- يا لها من كذبة!

10- هل تحب التفاح والبرتقال.

11- جاء مبكراً اليوم.

(c) Change the sentences into interrogative:

1- He speaks English at home.

2- We write Arabic in the school.

3- They go to the picture in the evening.

4- She sees her friend at the station.

5- I come here everyday.

6- The door opens in the day.

7- The fire burns all day.

8- He wants a telephone in his office.

Interrogative sentences:

1- ....

2- ....

3- ....

4- ....

5- ....

(ج) اجعل الجمل التالية في صيغة السؤال:

6- ....

7- ....

8- ....

ملاحظة: يجب أن تكون الكتابة واضحة وعلى السطر عند القيام بحل جميع التمارين. ولكي يكتسب الدارس الكتابة بشكل منظم وواضح، على الدَّارس أن يمارس الكتابة باستمرار ليكون خطّه جميلاً وسهلاً للقراءة.

(d) Change these sentences into Simple Future Tense:

(د) غيّر هذه الجمل إلى زمن المستقبل البسيط:

1- We always ask the same question.

2- I sometimes go the near station.

3- He eats an apple everyday.

4- She doesn't like to drink orange juice.

5- We don't leave the house today.

6- They start to write their old lesson.

7- She uses her new bicycle to go to her school.

8- Ali takes his tea at 7 o'clock in the morning.

9- Amira often reads her good story at home.

10- They visit their own farm every week.

Simple Future Tense:

زمن المستقبل البسيط:

1- ....

2- ....

3- ....

4- ....

5- ....

6- ....

7- ....

8- ....

9- ....

10- ....

(e) **Put the sentences into Simple Past Tense:**

1- I walk to my house on foot without my car.

2- He likes to read good stories at night.

3- They hear our music well from the window.

4- Lamya cooks good dinners.

5- He waits for me long hours at the school.

6- We run for the train at the station.

7- The cat drinks its water.

8- I teach English in the school.

9- Ali goes to his office everyday.

10- The policeman catches thieves.

Simple Past Tense:

1- ....

2- ....

3- ....

4- ....

5- ....

6- ....

7- ....

8- ....

9- ....

10- ....

(f) Change these sentences into Future Continuous (using going to):

(و) اجعل هذه الجمل في صيغة المستقبل المستمر:

1- I go home by car. ....

2- He reads our lessons. ....

3- We ride the horses. ....

4- She writes her letter. ....

5- They give him money. ....

6- Ali gives her the key. ....

7- Amira has a lesson. ....

8- Layla cooks the food. ....

9- We have a good house. ....

10- They play football. ....

(g) Put these verbs into Simple Past Tense:

(ز) ضع هذه الأفعال في زمن الماضي البسيط:

Present tense	Past tense	Present tense	Past tense
1- hear	....	1- speak	....
2- mean	....	2- know	....
3- go	....	3- sit	....
4- get	....	4- tell	....
5- drive	....	5- sleep	....

6- leave	....	6- play	....
7- write	....	7- fight	....
8- do – does	....	8- make	....
9- eat	....	9- love	....
10- take	....	10- like	....

(b) Translate the following verbs into English:

(ح) ترجم الأفعال التالية إلى الإنجليزية في زمن المضارع وفي زمن الماضي:

1-	1- سأل	....	1- يسأل
2-	2- ساعد	....	2- يساعد
3-	3- تأكد	....	3- يتأكد
4-	4- جاوب	....	4- يجاوب
5-	5- سمع	....	5- يسمع
6-	6- صدق	....	6- يصدق
7-	7- سلك	....	7- يسلك
8-	8- فك القيود	....	8- يفك
9-	9- حرر	....	9- يحرر
10-	10- نشر	....	10- ينشر

(i) Read the following passage and then translate it into Arabic:

(ط) اقرأ المقطع الآتي ثم ترجمه إلى العربية:

I know your house. It is near the big market. We went to visit it yesterday with our friends. We had some cups of juice. They were orange juice. Your father was reading a big map in his office. Afterwards, we took the train to go back home in town.

(i) Change the following passage into Past Simple Tense:

(ي) اجعل المقطع الآتي في الماضي البسيط:

Ali goes to his house to take his bag. He asks his mother about his bag. Afterwards, his mother gives him some bread for his breakfast. After the school, Ali takes his friends to visit his big farm of oranges and apples. His friends take some fruits to their homes.

(k) Write down the Past Simple Tense:

(ك) اكتب زمن الماضي البسيط في هذه السطور:

....

....

....

....

....

....

New words	الترجمة	New words	الترجمة
try	يجرب/يحاول	Anymore	بعد الآن
never	قط/أبداً/مطلقاً	Wrong	خطأ/غلط
behavior	سلوك/تصرّف		

اختبار رقم أربعة

Test No. Four

من تمرين رقم (1)

إلى تمرين رقم (4)

From Exercise (1)

to Exercise (4)

اختبار رقم (4)

تمرين: اختبار بين المضارع التام والماضي التام:

(1) Put in the correct verb instead of the verb in brackets:

(1) ضع الفعل الصحيح في الماضي بدلاً من الفعل المضارع بين قوسين:

1- She told me about the lesson after he (leave).

2- He (do) nothing before he saw me.

3- My friend enjoyed his food as soon as he (taste) it.

4- He thanked me for what I (do).

5- I (be) sorry that I had not come to see you.

6- After the teacher had (go), I (sit) down and (rest).

7- Did you read the letter after you (write) it?

8- As soon as you (go), I wanted to see you again.

9- They dressed after they (wash) their faces.

10- After I (have) heard the news, I (hurry) to see you.

11- She (tell) me her name after I (ask) her twice.

12- Before we (go) very far, we found that we (lose) our way.

13- After you (go), I went to sleep.

14- I read the book after I (finish) my work.

15- When they arrived, the dinner already (begin).

16- He died after he (be) ill a long time.

17- My friend Ali (not see) me for many years when I (meet) him at the station last week.

ملاحظة: إذا كنت قد استوعبت صيغ الأفعال المختلفة سيكون هذا التمرين الاختباري سهلاً عليك. أنظر

ترجمة الكلمات التالية من رقم (1) إلى رقم (12):

These are some (New Words) in Test Four:

1- nothing	لا شيء	7- hurry	يسرع
2- enjoyed	تمتع	8- twice	مرتين
3- as soon as	بمجرد	9- very far	بعيد جداً
4- thanked	شكر	10- ill	مريض
5- rest	يستريح	11- a long time	وقت طويل
6- dressed	لبس	12- when	عندما

(2) put in suitable prepositions in blank spaces: **(2) ضع حروف الجر المناسبة في الأماكن الشاغرة:**

1- I don't go .... School .... Sunday.

2- We stay .... winter .... home. We don't go ....

3- My father arrived .... Jordan .... Exactly 8 o'clock.

4- Try .... come .... 10 .... Friday morning.

5- I bought this car .... four thousand dollars.

6- He has not been here .... Monday.

7- You can write .... day .... a pencil.

8- There is no bus. You will have to go .... foot.

9- The teacher was sitting .... a desk .... the class.

10- He spoke .... me his hands   his pocket

11- They swim .... the sea.

12- Sugar is nice .... a cup of tea.

13- Knives are made .... metals.

14- I have no time .... help you today.

15- She goes .... foot to her school.

(3) **Make the following sentences from past simple tense to present perfect tense:** (4) اجعل الجمل التالية من زمن الماضي البسيط إلى زمن المضارع التام:

1- I wrote my homework last night.

2- He closed the door of the school just now.

3- They worked hard last week.

4- Did you put your exercise book in your bag?

5- Did you go to Dubai last month?

1- ....

2- ....

3- ....

4- ....

5- ....

(4) **Make the following sentences near future by using (going to):** (4) اجعل الجمل التالية في زمن المستقبل القريب وذلك باستعمال (going to) (سوف):

1- I will see him tomorrow.

2- He is leaving in few days.

3- She'll write to you later.

4- They are coming home soon.

317

اختبار رقم خمسة

Test No. Five

من تمرين رقم (1)

إلى تمرين رقم (4)

From Exercise (1)

to Exercise (4)

Test Number 5:

Put the verbs into the correct tense with other necessary changes:

First in the present tense.

Second in the past tense.

Third in the present perfect.

1- Ali (go) away every day to the market.

2- He (go) abroad last week with his car.

3- No, Amira isn't here. She just (go) out of home.

4- Layla (to come) downstairs when I (meet) her friend.

5- This man never (see) the picture.

6- You (see) my car?

7- Yes, I (see) it somewhere at the station.

8- I (see) him yesterday. He (sit) outside the school.

(1) First in the present tense:

1- ....

2- ....

3- ....

4- ....

5- ....

6- ....

7- ....

8- ....

اختبار رقم 5:

ضع الأفعال في الزمن الصحيح مع التغيّر اللازم:

(1) أولاً في المضارع البسيط.

(2) ثانياً في الماضي البسيط.

(3) في المضارع التام.

أولاً في المضارع البسيط:

(2) Second in the past tense:

ثانياً: في الماضي البسيط.

1- ....

2- ....

3- ....

4- ....

5- ....

6- ....

7- ....

8- ....

(3) Third in the present perfect:

ثالثاً: في المضارع التام:

1- ....

2- ....

3- ....

4- ....

5- ....

6- ....

7- ....

8- ....

Exercise (4):

تمرين (4):

Read these sentences very well and put the adverbs of the past into (tomorrow):

اقرأ هذه الجمل بطريقة جيدة وحاول أن تعيد الظروف من حالة الماضي إلى غداً:

1- The student read my new book (yesterday).

2- We have already bought the house.

3- They came here (last year).

4- The house did not cost too much.

5- He lived in that building (last time).

6- They did not work with us (yesterday).

7- I have been very busy (today).

8- All the family went to the party (last night).

9- She wrote a letter (three days ago).

10- The gardener has cut the tree (today).

1- ……………………………………………………………..

2- …………………………………………………………..

3- …………………………………………………………..

4- …………………………………………………………..

5- …………………………………………………………..

6- …………………………………………………………..

7- …………………………………………………………..

8- …………………………………………………………..

9- …………………………………………………………..

10- ……………..…………………………………………..

اختبار رقم ستة

Test No. Six

من تمرين رقم (1)

إلى تمرين رقم (9)

From Exercise (1)

to Exercise (9)

Test No (6):

اختبار رقم(6):

Exercise (1):

تمرين (1):

Ask a question for each word or words in brackets.

اجعل سؤالاً للكلمات ما بين القوسين

1- I want (her new car) today.

2- Amina ate (all the bread).

3- We were (in the school) this morning.

4- The sun was (very hot yesterday).

5- Ali is (15) years old today.

6- (My friend Ahmed) always helps his father.

7- (She came in) and (sat down).

8- That dress is (pretty) and (cheap also).

9- They did not go to school (because they were tired).

10- I am very angry today.

Exercise (2): Add the appropriate question-tag.

تمرين (2):

1- He is a teacher of English, ………………………………….... ?

2- He isn't a doctor of your school, ………………………….... ?

3- They are your friends, ………………………………......   ?

4- We have not seen him,………………………………….   ?

5- They are Lebanese, ………………………………….....   ?

6- You have a beautiful car, ………………………………   ?

7- She can write English, ………………………………...   ?

8- He cannot speak Arabic, ……………………………...   ?

9- You'll tell us your story, ……………………………...   ?

Exercise (3):   :(3) تمرين

Add a joining conjunction for each sentence.

1- He is kind. He is nice

2- He is a teacher. He does not read books.

3- She is tired. She doesn't want to go to school.

4- They don't eat meat. They are butchers.

5- Amina doesn't go to school. She is ill.

6- You can go. You must come early.

7- Your reading is good. It could be better.

8- Ahmed saw his friend. He was driving a new car.

9- Is this a good exercise? Is it bad?

10- Come at once. You will be late.

11- He didn't want to quarrel. He came to visit him.

12- I don't wish to go to school. It is very cold today.

13- I'll come to see you. I am very busy.

14- Come back. You can.

15- I'll wait here. You come with the ticket.

16- Look, you leap.

17- He had written the exercise. He went home.

18- Tell me. You finish reading the new book.

19- The students will get wet. It rains.

20- You will not speak English. He reads well.

لاحظ أن النقطة التي تفصل الجملتين هي مكان أداة الربط. لذلك يجب قراءة الجملتين جيداً قبل اختيار نوع الأداة التي تربطهما.

Exercise (4):.

Translate the following sentences into English

تمرين (4):

1- الغرفة التي أنت وأنا فيها الآن واسعة وجميلة.

2- الملابس التي ألبسها غالية ومصنوعة من قماش صوفي.

3- المرأة التي كانت بقربي هنا تتكلم الانجليزية جيد جداً.

4- الرجل الذي يشتغل في هذا المكتب سريع في عمله أما الشخص الذي يشتغل في الحانوت فبطيء في أعماله اليومية.

5- بيتنا الذي حول هذه البناية واسع وجميل ويوجد فيه أشجار كثيرة.

Translation:

1- ....

2- ....

3- ....

4- ....

5- ....

لاحظ أن لإعطاء الردود على هذه الأسئلة لا بد من مراجعة الدرس الخاص بها جيداً حتى يتمكن الدارس من الإجابة الصحيحة.

Exercise (5):   تمرين (5):

Put each of the following words in a sentence.

1- wind...

2- star ....

3- moon ....

4- light ....

5- nice ....

6- nicely ....

7- bad ....

8- badly ....

9- camel ....

10- ration ....

Use each word in a useful sentence.

1- journey... ..

2- by car ....

3- by plane ....

4- by train ....

5- lazy ....

6- the clock ....

7- slow up ....

8- drive ....

9- library ....

لاحظ أن الجملة لا بد أن تتكون من فاعل وفعل ومفعول به حتى تكون كاملة.

Exercise (7):.   :(7) تمرين

Answer the following questions:

1- What is the capital of Egypt?

2- What is the system of the government in Egypt?

3- What is the capital of Lebanon?

4- What form of government is in Lebanon?

5- Which country is not a republic?

Exercise (8):

تمرين (8):

Put a relative pronoun where is needed

1- This is Amina ………….. learns her lesson quickly.

2- The students have teachers ……. they like much.

3- My school ………. faces your house is closed today.

4- I found the books ……… I am interested to read.

5- I don't know …………he wants from the teacher.

6- They don't understand ……… they are saying.

7- This is the boy …….. book has been lost.

8- Where is the shop ………. sells newspapers here?

9- That man …………. you spoke to is my teacher.

Exercise (9):

تمرين(9):

Add an appropriate question-tag to each of the following sentences.

ضع عبارة للسؤال للجمل الآتية:

1- She has a beautiful house, ………………………………..?

2- They cannot do this exercise, ………………………….?

3- He must write his name, ………………………………?

4- We have seen him, ……………………………………?

5- He is Lebanese, ……………………………………….?

6- He came by train, …………………………………….?

7- We have eaten our food, ………………………………?

8- They received their books, …………………………….?

9- You had not slept, …………………………………....?

10- The children had good time, ………………………….?

اختبار رقم سبعة

Test No. Seven

من تمرين رقم (1)

إلى تمرين رقم (6)

From Exercise (1)

to Exercise (6)

Test No (7):

Exercise (1):

Translate into English:

اختبار رقم(7):

تمرين (1):

ترجم هذه الجمل إلى الإنجليزية:

(1) هذا الرجل صادق الوعد.

(2) اشترى المزرعة باسم أخيه.

(3) رأيت الرجل هو في صحة جيدة مرة أخرى.

(4) هو صاحب الحانوت الشرعي.

(5) أحاول دائماً أن أقرأ الجريدة بين السطور.

(6) حسناً.

(7) كان مفعماً بالنشاط.

Translation:

1- ....

2- ....

3- ....

4- ....

5- ....

6- ....

7- ....

Exercise (2):

Translate into Arabic:

1- This man is as good as his word.

2- He bought the farm in the name of his brother.

تمرين (2):ترجم إلى العربية:

3- I saw the man, he is all right again.

4- He is the right owner of this shop.

5- I always try to read the papers between the lines.

6- That's all right.

7- He was fresh.

Exercise (3):   تمرين (3):

Read and Answer. (The farmer and the mice).

Once there was a poor farmer who was always in trouble by the presence of plenty of rats in his hut. He then decided to go to the nearest town to get a cat for these rats. He was lucky for he found one strong black cat. He brought it, home and left it run about to try to catch these troublesome rats in the hut. But the rats which felt the presence of the cat in the hut, did not come out from their holes at all. However, when the cat was out of the farmer's hut, the rats, played, ate anything that came across and made a lot of noise in the hut.

Answer the following questions:

1- Why was the poor farmer in trouble?

2- Where were the rats?

3- What did the farmer do then?

4- Why did he go to the town?

5- What did he find?

1- ....

2- ....

3- ....

4- ....

5- ....

Exercise (4):

تمرين (4):

Make questions for these answers:

1- The farmer brought the cat at home.

2- He left the cat to run about.

3- To catch the mice.

4- The mice did not come out.

5- The mice played, ate and danced.

1- ………………………………………………

2- ………………………………………………

3- ………………………………………………

4- ………………………………………………

5- ………………………………………………

Exercise (5):

تمرين (5):

The interpretation of this short story:

شرح هذه الرواية القصيرة:

We understand that whenever a person who has some sort of an authority on other people, goes away or absents himself for sometime, the subordinates will start to make a lot of noise or will not work until he appears, like pupils in a classroom when their teacher is away for a short time.

Answer the following questions:

1- What do you understand from the story of the cat and the rats?

2- What do the subordinates do when the man of authority comes back?

3- Who does make a lot of noise like the subordinates?

1- ………………………………………………………

2- ....

3- ....

Exercise (6):   تمرين (6):

Make suitable sentences from these words:

1- How much

....

2- dear

....

3- cheap

....

4- permit

....

5- neither .... nor

....

6- nowadays

....

7- how

....

8- need

....

9- kind

....

10- advice

....

اختبار رقم ثمانية

Test No. Eight

من تمرين رقم (1)

إلى تمرين رقم (3)

From Exercise (1)

to Exercise (3)

Test No (8):	اختبار رقم(8):
Exercise (1):	تمرين (1):
Place each word in the blank space:	ضع كل كلمة في الفراغ المناسب

open – closed – smoking – sweeping – sleeping – inviting.

1- .... window

2- .... victory

3- .... eyed

4- .... car

5- .... offer

Exercise (2):	تمرين (2):
Translate into English:	ترجم إلى الإنجليزية:

لم يذهب إلى مكتب البريد اليوم – أرادني أن أترجم رسالتي إلى الإنجليزية – لم أره اليوم إطلاقاً – لم يجد النقود على المنضدة كما أخبرني اليوم صباحاً. أراد أن يذهب إلى تونس بنفسه. إني آسف لا أعرف اسمه جيداً – أرجو أن تساعدني على كتابته بالإنجليزية – شيء جميل جداً أن تزورني في المكتب في أي يوم تراه مناسباً لي ولك. أنا سعيد أن أراك في صحة جيدة. هل تتذكر أننا تقابلنا في السنة الماضية؟

Translation:

1- ....

2- ....

3- ....

4- ....

5- ....

6- ....

7- ....

تمرين (3):

صحح هذه الفقرة وذلك بوضع كلماتها في مكانها الأصلي:

Put the right word in its right place:

Are – wide – this morning – heard – sorry – to walk – to read – to stay – home.

.... the mountains high? Is the room ....? Did you read the newspaper ....? Have

you .... the news? I am .... that he is ill. We preferred .... than .... at

....

Answers to Tests

Answes of the test Number (1)

Exercise (a):

1- (a).

2- (the).

3- (the) – (a).

4- (the).

5- (a).

6- (an).

Exercise (b):

Proper Nouns	Nouns of Animals	Nouns Of Capitals	Nouns of Mountains
Amira	cat	Cairo	Sanine
Ahmad	dog	Damascus	Everest
Nouns of Rivers & Canals	Names of things	Abstract Nouns	Collective Nouns
The Nile	car	difficulty	sugar
Suez Canal	table	goodness	crew

Exercise (c):

Countable Nouns:

1- car.

2- bell.

3- class.

4- egg.

5- trousers.

Uncountable Nouns:

1- milk.

2- water.

3- butter.

4- cheese.

5- ice.

Exercise (d):

Translation.

1- The happy.

2- The weak.

3- The young.

4- The brave.

5- The rich.

6- This man is old.

7- That man is happy.

8- This woman is poor.

9- A Lebanese.

Exercise (e):

1- my.

2- your.

3- his.

4- her.

5- its.

6- our.

7- their.

Exercise (f):

1- Our farm is in our land.

2- They have their lessons in their houses.

3- They have their doctors in their schools.

4- The dogs have their food in their huts.

5- The cats have their balls in their huts.

6- Our mothers are in the house of our friend.

7- Their sisters are now in the classroom.

8- There are Englishmen in the farm.

9- These are their food.

10- Those are their houses in the big garden.

Exercise (g):

1- He – his radio.

2- she – her paper.

3- They – their ball.

4- They – their classroom.

5- They – their house.

1- mine.

2- his.

3- ours.

4- theirs.

5- mine.

6- mine.

7- mine.

8- mine.

9- his.

10- hers.

11- theirs.

12- its.

Answers To test Number (2):

Exercise (a):

1- (goes)

2- (write)

3- (carries)

4- (knows)

5- (tries)

Exercise (b):

1- I want a book. I want to write a letter.

2- Do you know the story of my life?

3- He sells oranges in his shop.

4- I do not speak English well.

5- They write their lessons at home.

6- We always ride our bicycles in the garden.

7- Tell me where are you going today?

8- I never eat outside home.

Exercise (c):

1- She does not get her newspaper every day.

2- They do not write their lessons in their houses.

3- He does not study everyday.

4- We do not go to sleep early.

5- You do not sit at home alone.

Exercise (d):

1- Do I go to ....?

2- Does my father ....?

3- Does Ali come ....?

4- Did he finish ....?

5- Did we wait for him ....?

Exercise (e):

1- I go to sleep early in the evening.

2- He comes to school very late everyday.

3- She goes to the hairdresser every week.

4- He tells his story to the officer.

5- The train runs to Saida every month.

Exercise (f):

The subject الفاعل	The object (Predicate) المفعول به
1- They (generally)	1- swim in this pool.
2- He (always)	2- wants some food for his dog.
3- Ali (often)	3- knows his lessons well.
4- Amira (sometimes)	4- wishes to go to France.
5- The teacher.	5- teaches English in this room.

Exercise (g):

لاحظ أن عملية تكوين الأفعال المنفردة في جمل مفيدة يتوقف على المطالعة المستمرّة:

1- I believe in God.

2- The boy will care for his books.

3- My lesson consists of ten pages.

4- Cats usually hate dogs. I don't hate him.

5- I like to know my lesson very well.

6- All books contain good information.

7- The teacher desires your presence in the class.

8- I do not hear any news in the day.

9- They wish to travel in the country.

10- We study English at home.

Exercise (h):

1- I believed in God in everything I do.

2- The boy would care for his books.

3- My lesson consisted of ten pages.

4- Cats usually hated dogs.

5- I liked to know my lesson very well.

6- All books contained good information.

7- The teacher desired your presence in the class.

8- I did not hear any news today.

9- They wished to travel in the country.

10- We studied English at home.

Exercise (i):

1- He always goes to school early.

2- I am finishing my work now.

3- She learns Arabic every morning.

4- They are going out at the present time.

5- We told the story last week.

6- Ali is playing music now.

7- Layla is studying English now.

8- Lamya went to her friend yesterday.

9- He is coming to work very soon.

Exercise (j):

1- I am going home now.

2- He is writing his lesson at the present time.

3- We are doing our work in our field.

4- They are learning English in this class.

5- She is telling her lesson to the teacher.

Exercise (k):

1- I was going home then.

2- He was writing his lesson at that time.

3- We were doing our work in our field.

4- They were learning English in this class.

5- She was telling her lesson to the teacher.

Exercise (l):

1- Smoking is very dangerous to the health.

2- He started studying his lessons.

3- I began reading a new book of history.

4- I like swimming in the pool.

5- Do you mind speaking slow?

6- They always like playing football.

7- She does not mind writing her address.

8- We don't mind giving help to the poor.

9- He loves eating oranges everyday.

10- I don't like having much homework

Answers to test number (3):

Exercise (a):

1- I shall be naming ………………

2- We shall be leading ……………

3- He will be deciding …………….

4- She will be visiting ……………..

5- You will be admiring ……………

6- He will be assuring ………...

7- I shall be going …………….

8- We shall be going …………...

9- They will be appreciating ………….

10- The train will be arriving ………….

Exercise (b):

1- He has not gone to his office today.

2- They don't speak English well.

3- I didn't see him today.

4- He didn't find the money on the table.

5- We don't want him to go to France.

6- You can't buy this car.

7- The weather is hot in summer and cold in winter.

8- He is generous because he is rich.

9- What a lie!

10- Do you like apples and oranges.

11- He came early today.

Exercise (c):

1- Does he ……….?

2- Do we ....?

3- Do they ....?

4- Does she ....?

5- Do I ....?

6- Does the door ....?

7- Does the fire ....?

8- Does he find ....?

Exercise (d):

1- We shall always ....

2- I shall sometimes ....

3- He will eat ....

4- She will not like ....

5- We shall not leave ....

6- They will start ....

7- She will use her ....

8- Ali will take ....

9- Amira will often read ....

10- They will visit their ....

Exercise (e):

1- I walked ....

2- He liked ....

3- They heard ....

4- Lamya cooked ....

5- He waited ....

6- We ran ....

7- The cat drank ....

8- I taught ……………….

9- Ali went ……………...

10- The policeman caught ………..

Exercise (f)

1- I am going home by car.

2- He is going to read ………….

3- We are going to ride ………….

4- She is going to write …………….

5- They are going to give …………..

6- Ali is going to give …………….

7- Amira is going to have …………

8- Layla is going to cook ……….

9- We are going to have ………….

10- They are going to play ………..

Exercise (g):

1- heard	1- spoke
2- meant	2- knew
3- went	3- sat
4- got	4- told
5- drove	5- slept
6- left	6- played
7- wrote	7- fought
8- did	8- made
9- ate	9- loved
10- took	10- liked

Exercise (h):

1- ask	1- asked
2- help (assist)	2- helped – assisted
3- assure	3- assured
4- answer	4- answered
5- hear	5- heard
6- believe	6- believed
7- behave	7- behaved
8- unfasten	8- unfastened
9- unfetter	9- unfettered
10- unfold	10- unfolded

Exercise (i):

أعرف منزلك وهو قريب من السوق الكبير. وقد ذهبنا لزيارته أمس مع أصدقائنا. كنا قد أخذنا بعض أكواب من العصير. فكانت عصير برتقال. كان والدك يقرأ في خريطة كبيرة في مكتبه. وبعد ذلك أخذنا القطار للرجوع إلى المنزل في المدينة.

Exercise (j):

Ali went to his house to take his bag. He asked his mother about his bag. Afterwards, his mother gave him some bread for his breakfast. After the school, Ali took his friends to visit his big farm of oranges and apples. His friends took some fruits to their homes.

Answers to Test Number (4)

Exercise (1):

1- .... after he had left.

2- He had done ....

3- .... as he had tasted it.

4- .... for what I have done.

5- I was sorry that ....

6- .... had gone, I sat down and rested.

7- .... the letter after you had written it?

8- As soon as you had gone, ...

9- .... after they had washed.

10- After I had heard ...., I hurried ....

11- She told .... after I had asked ....

12- Before we went ...., we found that we had lost ....

13- After you had gone, I ....

14- .... after I had finished ....

15- ...., the dinner already had begun.

16- .... after he had been ill ....

17- My friend Ali had not seen me for many years when I met him at the .... last week.

Exercise (2):

1- .... to .... on ....

2- .... in .... at .... we .... out.

3- .... in .... at ....

4- Try to come at 10 on ....

5- .... for ....

6- .... since ....

7- .... today with a pencil.

8- .... to go on foot.

9- .... by a desk in the class.

10- .... to me with .... in his ....

11- .... in the sea ....

12- .... is nice in a cup of tea.

13- .... of metals.

14- .... to help you ....

15- She goes on foot ....

Exercise (3):

1- I have

2- He has just closed the door of the school.

3- They have worked hard.

4- Have you put your exercise book in your bag?

5- Have you gone to Dubai?

Exercise (4):

1- I am going to see him tomorrow.

2- He is going to leave in a few days.

3- She is going to write to you later.

4- They are going to come home soon.

5- We are going to have dinner later.

Answers to test Number (5):

Exercise: Simple Present Tense (1):

1- Ali goes away everyday to the market.

2- He goes abroad every week with his car.

3- No, Amira isn't here. She is out of home.

4- Layla is coming downstairs to meet her friend.

5- This man does not see the picture.

6- Do you see my car?

7- Yes, I always see it somewhere at the station.

8- I see him every day. He sits outside the school.

Simple past Tense (2):

1- Ali went away yesterday.

2- He went abroad last week.

3- No, Amira wasn't here. She was out of home.

4- Layla was coming downstairs to meet her friend.

5- This man did not see the picture.

6- Did you see my car?

7- Yes, I always saw it somewhere at the station.

8- I saw him yesterday. He sat outside the school.

Present Perfect Tense (3):

1- Ali has gone away today.

2- He has gone abroad this week.

3- No, Amira has not been here. She has gone out of home.

4- Layla has come downstairs to meet her friend.

5- This man has not seen the picture.

6- Have you seen my car?

7- Yes, I have always seen it somewhere at the station.

8- I have seen him today. He has sat outside the school.

Exercise (4):

1- The student will read my new book tomorrow.

2- We will buy the house tomorrow.

3- They will come here next year.

4- The house will not cost too much.

5- He will live in that building next time.

6- They will not work with us tomorrow.

7- I will be very busy tomorrow.

8- All the family will go to the party tomorrow night.

9- She will write a letter tomorrow.

10- The gardener will cut the tree tomorrow.

Answers to test Number (6):

Exercise (1):

1- What do you want?

2- What did Amina eat?

3- Where were you this morning?

4- How was the sun yesterday?

5- How old is Ali today?

6- Who always helps his father?

7- Who came in? And what did she do?

8- How is that dress? And how much is it?

9- Why didn't they go to school?

10- What is the matter with you?

Exercise (2):

1- .... isn't he?

2- .... is he?

3- .... aren't they?

4- .... have you?

5- .... aren't they?

6- .... haven't you?

7- .... can't she?

8- .... can he?

9- .... won't you?

Exercise (3):

1- He is kind and nice.

2- He is a teacher but he does not read books.

3- She is tired therefore she does not want to go to school.

4- They don't eat meat yet they are butchers.

5- Amina does not go to school for she is ill.

6- You can go but you must come early.

7- Your reading is good still it could be better.

8- Ahmed saw his friend who was driving a new car.

9- Is this a good exercise or is it bad?

10- Come at once otherwise you will be late.

11- He didn't want to quarrel, besides he came to visit him.

12- I don't want to go to school for it is very cold today.

13- I'll come to see you however I am very busy.

14- Come back when you can.

15- I'll wait here until you come with the ticket.

16- Look before you leap.

17- He had written the exercise after he went home.

18- Tell me when you finish reading the new book.

19- The student will get wet if it rains.

20- You will not speak English unless you read well.

Exercise (4):

1- The room which we are in now is wide and beautiful.

2- The clothes which I wear are expensive and are made of woolen cloth.

3- The woman who was here beside me speaks English very well.

4- The man who works in this office is quick in his job but the person who works in the shop is slow.

5- Our house which is round this building is wide and beautiful and there are a lot of trees in it.

Exercise (5):

1- I tried to wind a clock. A shelter from the wind.

2- He is the star of this football team.

3- The moon is not clear tonight.

4- The sun gives light to the earth.

5- This is a nice place to go to visit.

6- He writes his exercises nicely.

7- Never try to do bad things to other persons.

8- He speaks English badly.

9- A camel is a man's companion in the desert.

10- They forgot to give the poor man his right ration.

Exercise (6):

1- He made a good journey to France.

2- I always like to travel by car.

3- My brother wants to go to France by plane.

4- Whenever my friend is in Italy, he likes to travel by train.

5- The teacher does not like lazy students in his class.

6- The pupils are watching the clock of the school.

7- The policeman told me to slow down when I am in town.

8- Drive always slow past schools.

9- I have a good library at home. It is full of books.

Exercise (7):

1- The capital of Egypt is Cairo.

2- The system of the government in Egypt is republic.

3- The capital of Lebanon is Beirut.

4- The form of the government in Lebanon is republic.

5- The state of Jordan is not a republic. It is a monarchy.

Exercise (8):

1- This is Amina who learns her lessons quickly.

2- The students have teachers whom they like much.

3- My school which faces your house is closed today.

4- I found the books which I am interested to read.

5- I don't know what he wants from the teacher.

6- They don't understand what they are saying.

7- This is the boy whose book has been lost.

8- Where is the shop which sells newspapers here?

9- That man to whom you spoke is my teacher.

Exercise (9):

1- She has a beautiful house, hasn't she?

2- They cannot do this exercise, can they?

3- He must write his name, mustn't he?

4- We have seen him, haven't we?

5- He is Lebanese, isn't he?

6- He came by train, didn't he?

7- We have eaten our food, haven't we?

8- They received their books, didn't they?

9- You had not slept, had you?

10- The children had good time, hadn't they?

Answers to test Number (7):

Exercise (1):

1- This man is as good as his word.

2- He bought the farm in the name of his brother.

3- I saw the man, he is all right again.

4- He is the right owner of this shop.

5- I always try to read the papers between the lines.

6- That's all right.

7- He was fresh.

Exercise (2):

(1) هذا الرجل صادق الوعد.

(2) اشترى المزرعة باسم أخيه.

(3) رأيت الرجل هو في صحة جيدة مرة أخرى.

(4) هو صاحب الحانوت الشرعي.

(5) أحاول دائماً أن أقرأ الجريدة بين السطور.

(6) حسناً.

(7) كان مفعماً بالنشاط.

Exercise (3):

1- Because of the presence of plenty of mice in his hut.

2- The mice were in his hut.

3- He then decided to go to the nearest town.

4- He went to the town to get a car.

5- He found one strong black cat.

Exercise (4):

1- What did the farmer bring at home?

2- What did he have to run about?

3- Why did the farmer leave the cat to run – about?

4- What did the mice do?

5- What did the mice do when the cat was out of the hut?

Exercise (5):

1- We understand that whenever a person of some sort of authority on other people is absent for sometime, the subordinate will not work, until he appears again in his place.

2- The subordinates start to work again each one in his place as if nothing had happened.

3- The pupils in their classrooms when the teacher is away from the classroom.

Exercise (6):

Suitable sentences:

1- How much is this car?

2- This car is very dear.

3- This house is cheap.

4- Please permit to open this letter.

5- My father told me neither I nor my brother can travel to London.

6- Nowadays all people travel by cars.

7- How is your father today?

8- I am not in need of this horse.

9- You are very kind. What kind of story is this?

10- Take my advice never leave till tomorrow that which you can do today.

Answers to test Number (8):

Exercise (1):

1- A closed window.

2- A sweeping victory.

3- Open eyed.

4- A sleeping car.

5- An inviting offer.

Exercise (2):

He did not go to the post office today. He wanted me to translate my letter into English. I did not see him at all today. He did not find the money on the table as he told me this morning. He wanted to go to Tunis by himself. I am sorry, I don't know his name very well. Please, help me to write it in English. It is very nice to visit me in the office any day you see it suitable for me and for you. I am happy to see you in good health. Do you remember we met last year?

Exercise (3):

Are the mountains high? Is the room wide? Did you read the newspaper this morning? Have you read the news? I am sorry that he is ill. We preferred to walk than to stay at home.

Answers:

Exercise 1 – page (7):

1- a	9- the
2- a	10- the
3- an.	11- the
4- an	12- 16
5- an	13- a
6- a	14- a
7- a	15- the
8- the	16- the

Exercise 2 – page (12):

(a)	(b)	(c)	(d)
Ahmed	cat	Tripoli	Gibraltar
Sara	cow	Rome	The Atlas
Nadia	camel	Rabat	The Alps
Taghreed	cock	Kuwait	Everest
(e)	(f)	(g)	(h)
The Nile	desk	difficulty	team
Mississippi	table	hungry	salt
Amazon	key	goodness	crew
Suez Canal	car		cloth

Exercise 3 – page (15):

(a)	(a)
1- s	5- s
2- s	6- s
3- s	7- s
4- لا تجمع	

(b)	(b)
1- s	24- ies
2- لا تجمع	25- s
3- s	26- s
4- s	27- لا تجمع
5- es	28- ies
6- لا تجمع	29- ies
7- ies	30- s
8- es	31- s
9- s	32- ies
10- s	33- s
11- ies	34- s
12- s	35- ves
13- ies	36- s
14- s	37- s
15- es	38- s
16- ies	39- لا تجمع

17- es	40- es
18- s	41- s
19- ies	42- ies
20- s	43- s
21- s	44- لا تجمع
22- s	45- ves
23- s	

Exercise 4 – page (26):

1- my	mine	me
2- our	ours	us
3- your	yours	you
4- your	yours	you
5- your	yours	you
6- your	yours	you
7- your	yours	you
8- your	yours	you
9- his	his	him
10- her	hers	her
11- its	its	it
12- they	theirs	them

Exercise 5 – page (31): (a)

1- is	6- are
2- are	7- are

3- is	8- are
4- is	9- are
5- is	10- are

Exercise 5 – page (31): (b)

1- Yes, this is a cat.	5- Yes, we are men.
2- Yes, I am a teacher.	6- Yes, they are poor.
3- Yes, she is a nurse.	7- Yes, they are strong.
4- Yes, this is Lebanese.	8- Yes, we are rich men.

Exercise 5 – page (32): (c)

1- No, he is not a woman.	5- No, we are not engineers.
2- No, this is not a cat.	6- No, they are not housekeepers.
3- No, that is not a boy.	7- No, this is not a pencil.
4- No, we are not American.	

Exercise 6 (a) – page (33):

1- was	6- were
2- were	7- were
3- was	8- were
4- was	9- were
5- was	10- were

Exercise 6 (b) – page (34):

1- Yes, this was a cat.	5- Yes, we were doctors.

2- Yes, you were a doctor.

3- Yes, she was a girl.

4- Yes, he was Syrian.

6- Yes, they were poor.

7- Yes, they were strong.

8- Yes, they were rich men.

Exercise 7 (a) – page (43):

1- I shall go to …..

2- We shall have …..

3- They will be teachers……

4- We shall be happy…..

5- I will have …….

6- We shall be there tomorrow……

7- They will have ……

8- It will have …….

9- I will be tired……

10- They will be there today.

Exercise 7 (b) – page (44):

1- I won't be a farmer.

2- You won't be a teacher.

3- He won't have a ball.

4- She won't have a car.

5- We won't have our farm.

6- They won't have their bicycles.

Exercise 8 (a) – page (48):

1- Have I a house?

2- Have we a picture?

3- Has he a pencil?

4- Has she a copybook?

5- Has it its food?

6- Have you pens?

7- Have they newspapers?

Exercise 8 (b) – page (49):

1- I have not a picture.

2- We have not any house.

3- He has not a room.

4- She has not a dress.

5- It has not a ball.

6- You have not a map.

7- They have not their map.

Exercise 8 (c) – page (50):

1- I hadn't a picture.

2- We hadn't any house.

3- He hadn't a ball.

4- She hadn't a magazine.

5- It hadn't a ball.

6- You hadn't a map.

7- They hadn't their book.

Exercise 9 (a) – page (58):

1- (goes) slowly.

2- (plays).

3- (runs).

4- (live).

5- (comes).

6- (studies).

7- (eats).

8- (writes).

9- (studies).

10- (helps)

11- (does).

12- (hurts).

13- (takes).

14- (swims).

15- (drives).

16- (understands).

17- (read).

18- (wakes).

19- (cleans).

20- (speaks).

Exercise 9 (b) – page (60):

1- I do not play football everyday.

2- We do not write our letters at home.

3- He does not know his name very well.

4- She does not sell apples everyday.

5- He does not wish to go to London.

6- It does not play with its ball.

Exercise 10 (a) – page (64):

1- I did not go to sleep early.

2- He did not come home soon.

3- She did not go to her home.

4- The dog did not eat its food.

5- We did not write our letters.

6- They did not sit at home.

7- They did not go out last night.

8- Ali did not read his lesson.

9- He did not tell his story well.

10- They did not get their money.

11- Layla did not study her lesson.

12- She did not play with the ball.

13- I did not hope to come today.

14- She did not take her bicycle.

Exercise 10 (b) – page (65):

1- Did I go to sleep early?

2- Did he finish his lesson?

3- Did she like her ball?

4- Did the dog eat its food?

5- Did we wait for him her?

6- Did they learn the way?

7- Did you laugh at him?

8- Did they go out last night?

9- Did he tell his story well?

10- Did they get their money?

11- Did Layla study her lesson?

12- Did she play with the ball?

13- Did I hope to come today?

14- Did she take her bicycle?

Exercise 11 – page (67):

1- (went).

2- (came).

3- (went).

4- (is going to).

5- (wrote).

6- (sat).

7- (went).

8- (will read).

9- (is going to).

10- (ran).

11- (shall).

12- (wrote).

13- (knew).

14- (wished).

15- (payed).

16- (took).

17- (studied).

18- (drove).

Exercise 12 – page (73):

1- (goes).

2- (am fishing).

3- (learns).

4- (are going out).

5- (are telling).

6- (plays).

7- (is studying).

8- (take).

9- (is coming).

Exercise 13 (a) – page (77):

1- She is sitting …..

2- We are learning ….

3- You are speaking ….

4- I am going to …..

5- They are playing ….

6- Ali is taking …..

7- Layla is telling …..

8- They are drinking …..

Exercise 13 (b) – page (78):

1- She was sitting …..

2- We were learning …..

3- You were speaking …..

4- I was going to ……

5- They were playing …..

6- Ali was taking ……

7- Yousef and Salwa were reading …..

8- They were drinking …..

Exercise 14 (a) – page (96):

1- I am digging ………..

2- We are doing ………

3- You are drawing ………….

4- She is drinking ……………

5- It is driving out ……………

6- You are dwelling ………….

7- He is dreaming ……………

8- They are eating ……………

Exercise 14 (b) – page (96):

1- I did not dig ………..

2- We did not …………

3- You did not draw ………

4- She did not drink ………..

5- It did not drive out ………..

6- You did not dwell ....

7- He did not dream ....

8- They did not eat ....

Exercise 15 – page (103):

1- .... in the river

2- .... to .... to ....

3- .... lie in .... to ....

4- .... in Beirut for sometime.

5- .... in .... but .... at Saida.

6- .... in my exercise for today.

7- .... up at ....

8- .... in the cinema.

9- .... to school with his ....

10- .... in these chairs by the fire.

11- .... to school ....

12- .... at the school.

13- .... about. The sky is over our heads.

14- .... off .... on the table.

15- .... on .... Come with me ....

16- .... with his brother by the river ....

17- .... on Friday .... with you.

18- .... is upstairs .... His .... is downstairs.

19- .... to the .... with ....

20- .... to the class about ....

Exercise 16 (a) (question) – page (111):

1- Can you read English well?

2- Are you able to read English well?

3- Could you read English well?

4- Were you able to read English well?

5- Will you be able to read English well next week?

6- Would you be able to read English if you did all the exercises?

7- Will he be able to read English next week?

8- Would he be able to read English next week?

9- Will the tree bear fruit next month?

10- Will he tell me about it next day?

11- Would he tell me about it next day?

12- Have you found my book in your desk?

13- Will you hear me? Is this reading right?

14- Must they answer all the exercises well?

15- Will you answer this question after the lesson?

16- Will you find the pupils in the class?

17- Will this story be forgotten?

18- Will you be able to tell me the whole story?

19- Could he tell me the story?

20- Ought the train be here now?

21- Must he be patient?

22- Will they be all soldiers next moth?

Exercise 16 (b) (negative) – page (111):

1- I cannot ……….

2- I am not ……….

3- I could not ………

4- I was not ………..

5- I shall not be ……….

6- I should not be ………. if I did not ………..

7- He will not be ………..

8- He would not ………….. if he did not ………….

9- The tree will not ……………

10- He will not ………..

11- He would not ………

12- I have not found ……….

13- I shall not ……………

14- They must not ………….

15- I shall not ………….

16- You will not find ………..

17- This story will not ………..

18- You will not be ………….

19- He could not ……………

20- The train ought not ………..

21- You must not be ……………

22- They will not be ……………

Exercise 17 (a) – page (132):

1- better	best
2- more beautiful	most beautiful
3- less	least
4- more difficult	most difficult
5- more than	most of
6- more dangerous	most dangerous
7- nicer	nicest
8- wider	widest
9- more useful	most useful
10- stronger	strongest
11- happier	happiest
12- worse	worst
13- more greedy	most greedy
14- farther	farthest
15- more	most
16- more expensive	most expensive
17- older	oldest

Exercise 17 (b) – page (134):

Negative	**Interrogative**
1- I have not any	Have you any book.......?
2- He has not any	Has he any money.........?
3- There is not any	Is there any dog ....?
4- I have not any	Have you any work ....?
5- They can't do anything	Can they do anything......?

6- She didn't tell to anybody ......   Did she tell to anybody ....?

7- No one has taken ....   Has anyone taken..........?

8- I don't want any ....   Do you want any ....?

9- There is nobody.   Is there anybody here?

10- We don't want to read any ....   Do you want to read any......?

Exercise 18 – page (148):

1- The boy's book.

2- The boys' books.

3- The women's names.

4- The cat's eyes.

5- The teacher's advice.

6- The tailor's shop.

7- The farmer's wife.

8- I want the pay of my month.

9- The food of the dog is bad.

Exercise 19 (a) – page (151):

1- mine, yours, herself.

2- mine, yours, myself.

3- her, herself.

4- myself.

5- ourselves.

6- yourself.

7- mine, myself.

8- herself.

9- yourselves, your.

Exercise 19 (b) – page (151):

1- any.

2- some.

3- some.

4- some.

5- some.

6- any.

7- some.

8- any.

9- some.

10- some.

11- any.

Exercise 20 (a) – page (159):

1- who.

2- which of.

3- where .

4- which.

5- what.

6- what.

7- where.

8- what.

9- which.

10- whose.

Exercise 20 (b) – page (159):

1- which.

2- whom.

3- which.

4- who.

Exercise 21 – page (161):

1- Who has ....?

2- Who has ....?

3- What has ....?

4- Whom do ....?

5- What is ....?

6- Who is ....?

7- Who has ....?

8- Whom did ....?

9- What do ....?

10- Who ate the cake?

11- Where were you today?

12- What had you last week?

13- How old are you today?

14- How was the sun yesterday?

15- How old is Ahmed today?

Exercise 22 – page (164):

1- He is a doctor   , isn't he?

2- ...., is he?

7- Their best friends and some of their neighbours will come to the birthday party.

8- His aunts have six children.

9- They will celebrate the birthday party in the evening.

10- Ahmed's brother will receive his presents after they all had enjoyed the birthday party.

Exercise 26 – page (193):

1- Ali lives in the country.

2- Because it is hot in the town.

3- The sun is rare in Europe.

4- Ali's family spent three months.

5- Ali's family likes to remain at home.

6- To spend (spending) a lot of money isn't fair in these difficult days in Ali's opinion.

Exercise 27 – page (197):

1- Meat is eaten by him everyday in this restaurant.

2- A new car was being bought by her yesterday.

3- Written English is being taught by me to you.

4- A warm welcome was given by Ali.

5- The new house will be shown by them to her today.

6- The gardens will be cleaned by the farmers.

7- Three boys have been seen by us near the school.

8- The exercise is written well by her.

9- The window was broken by you.

10- A new book was given by his brother.

Exercise 28 – page (198):

1- The wind blew the trees down.

2- The cat catches the mouse.

3- The clouds hid the sky.

4- I could not forgive him.

5- You must not forget this lesson.

6- You all are listening to the lecture.

7- I will give him some important books.

8- They took away the old books from the house.

9- He can tell the lesson easily.

10- You will receive this book tomorrow.

Exercise 29 – page (214):

1- The student said that lesson was not easy at all that day.

2- The teacher says that I must do the exercise that day.

3- I said to my father that I always read my lessons for I want to pass the examination.

4- Layla says to her mother that she does not like to go to swim that day.

5- The boys said that they could read and write well.

6- The student said to his father that he had told him a new story.

7- My father told me to take my bag with me to school everyday.

8- The servant said that he did not know to cook the fish at all.

9- The farmer has told his children that they all lazy boys and that they must work hard in that farm if they wanted to be well-off.

Exercise 30 – page (215):

1- I asked my friend if his school was far away.

2- The boy asked his father if there were one thousand dirhams in a dinar.

3- He asked me whether I did not go to school on Friday.

4- His friend asked if I stayed at home in winter and I did not go out.

5- The boy asked if my father had arrived in Morocco the day before.

6- He asked if he had not been there since Monday.

7- He asked whether knives were made of metals.

8- The teacher asked if I could tell him why I had left the class.

9- The teacher asked the student if it was true that lesson was easy.

10- The teacher asked the student whether his mother had been glad of his success.

11- He asked if he had some of these fruits.

12- He asked if he had the new tickets of the train.

13- The man asked if she had got some flowers in the garden.

14- His father asked if he had got some flowers in the garden.

15- They asked if there was some time for another cup of tea.

16- My friend asked who had gone with me to Paris.

17- Ali asked Ahmed which of those lessons was the best.

18- The student asked where was his place in that class.

19- The foreigner asked the driver which bus went to Tripoli.

20- The man asked what was wrong with the clock.

21- The policeman asked Ali what was his friend's name and why he was without the driving license.

22- The tourist asked the policeman which was the nearest way for them to the station.

23- The teacher asked the pupil what was the matter with him that day and asked him if he had not done his homework.

24- The inspector asked Mustafa which of those students there was his brother.

25- The shopkeeper asked the woman there which dress was that, his or hers.

Exercise 31 – page (217):

1- He begged him to go away from that place.

2- She prayed the student to come soon.

3- The teacher ordered the servant to close the school.

4- His father told the teacher that his son would be absent that day.

5- The teacher advised all students in the class to read slowly so they could understand their lessons well.

6- The director ordered the employee to bring there all the files of the hotel.

7- Ali told his friend Ahmed to go with him to watch the football match with his family that day.

8- The student's father told the teacher that his son did not know to spell his proper name.

9- His neighbor told his friend not to take ever the new car without permission.

10- The father told his son not to drive his car at night.

Exercise 32 – page (218):

1- The shopkeeper said with regret that he had lost his money that day.

2- The tourist said with satisfaction that the place of pictures was beautiful.

3- The teacher said with pleasure that the student was nice.

4- Ali said with sorrow that that man was ugly.

5- The director of the museums greeted all the new tourists who had come to visit that museum that day.

6- Ali's mother said with deep sorrow that he had cut himself with that dirty knife.

7- The policeman said with anger to the owner of that hotel what a dirty place that was.

8- I said with deep regret that I had forgotten to bring the lesson with me.

9- He shouted to the policeman to help him.

10- The owner of the car said with regret to the driver that he was fool that day.

11- The man there said with sorrow that he had lost his bag of money on his way to the station that day.

12- The foreigner shouted to the officer that the thief was there standing near the red car.

13- The host greeted respectfully all the guests when they had arrived to his new house.

14- The trainer of the blue football team said with deep regret that it was too bad when he had heard the news of the defeat of his team the day before.

15- The soldiers shouted long live the general.

16- The Arabs everywhere shouted with great satisfaction and joy that they had won the war against their arch enemy in 1973.

17- The cook cried with sorrow that he had made a mistake that day for he had forgotten to prepare the food for the new guests that day.

18- The students said with regret that the teacher had not explained that important lesson to them that day.

Exercise 33 – page (230):

1- He wants to know if Ahmed is interested to study English.

2- English is the main subject of conversation.

3- Because he may wish to travel abroad.

4- No, it is used for many other things.

5- It is used for translation.

6- The lack of understanding each other's language.

Exercise 34 – page (230):

1- To what are you interested?

2- What is your wish?

3- What is not good in your opinion?

4- What is really useful to know?

5- Why did other people study the Arabic language in the past?

6- What leads to a cordial relation?

Exercise 35 (a) – page (240):

1- swimming

2- getting

3- coming

4- wanting

5- hearing

6- knowing

7- wishing

8- driving

9- doing

10- selling

Exercise 35 (b) – page (241):

1- told

2- run

3- carried

4- taught

5- eaten

6- spoken

7- tried

8- ridden

9- fought

10- lived

Exercise 36 – page (241):

1- How much does this house cost?

2- Permit me to do this good work.

3- I have no knowledge of the matter at all.

4- Do you want to know the case?

5- Poverty is not a shame.

6- But it is shame to be a lazy man.

7- I have nothing to do with the matter at all.

8- I want neither this house nor that farm.

9- Do always good to others. You will be happy.

10- I shall wait until the man comes here.

Exercise 37 – page (242):

1- …………….. his new bicycle tomorrow.

2- …………….. to the school with his bicycle tomorrow.

3- …………….. absent tomorrow for she is very busy.

4- …………….. written the lesson on the black board.

5- …………….. not seen the new patient.

6- …………….. seen the patient sitting in his bed.

7- …………….. forget to read our lesson tomorrow.

8- Will they come to the museum today?

9- …………….. with you to our friend's house.

10- This book is yours.

11- …………….. went to London yesterday.

12- They will go without him for he has a lot of lessons.

13- I do not need him.

14- I am not in need of him.

15- …………… I shall be with you in the garden.

16- I live in Beirut and it is near this street.

17- He is going to read his lessons in his room.

18- She is going to study her story after tomorrow.

19- I am going to see him tonight in his house.

20- We are going to write a letter to our friend Ali.

21- Are you going to drive the new bicycle today?

Exercise 38 (a) – page (245):

1- They are sitting in the classroom.

2- Because they had given the lessons.

3- They had given their lessons to their students.

4- I think they are talking about the next examinations.

5- The standard of the examinations will be for the secondary school.

Exercise 38 (b) – page (246):

1- About what is the conversation?

2- When will the examinations be?

3- How do you think will the examinations be?

4- How are the examinations prepared?

5- From what does success come?

Exercise 39   – page (263):

1- Ahmed wants to know from Ali where the post office is in that town.

2- He wants to send it by airmail.

3- He wants to send the letter to his father.

4- Because his father has not sent any news about him.

5- His father is in Paris.

6- Ahmed's father is in Paris to study.

7- A telegram is quicker than a letter.

8- Ali's opinion was wonderful. It was good.

فهرس الموضوعات

Table of Contents

T0102977

Printed in the United States
By Bookmasters